INVISIBLE CITIZENS

British public opinion and the future of broadcasting

Dr David Morrison

A Report from the
Broadcasting Research Unit

October 1986

British Library Cataloguing in Publication Data

Morrison, David
  Invisible citizens: British public opinion and the future of broadcasting. —
  (Broadcasting Research Unit monograph, ISSN 0905-8716; 1)
  1. Broadcasting — Great Britain — Public opinion
  I. Title   II. Series 384.54′0941   HE8689.9.G7

  ISBN 0-86196-111-0

Published by
John Libbey & Company Ltd.
80/84 Bondway, London SW8 1SF, England (01) 582 5266
John Libbey Eurotext Ltd.
6 rue Blanche, 92120 Montrouge, France (1) 47 35 85 52

Printed in Great Britain by
Whitstable Litho Ltd., Whitstable, Kent

6.95

WITHDRAWN

Invisible citizens

British public opinion
and the future
of broadcasting ⅋ A

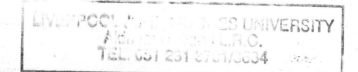

For Kirstie.

INVISIBLE CITIZENS

BRITISH PUBLIC OPINION AND THE FUTURE OF BROADCASTING

Contents   *Page*

Introduction 1

Public Opinion Research and the Future of Broadcasting 1

Public Opinion and Financing Broadcasting: Television 2

Public Opinion and Financing Broadcasting: Radio 8

Market Research and Social Research 11

Remembering Reith (1) 12

A Question of Quality 14

A Question of Pleasure 18

A Question of Loyalty 19

Remembering Reith (2) 21

Multi-dimensional Man 24

Conclusion 29

Tables 33

Appendix I 77

Appendix II 80

Appendix III – Factor Analysis and Factor Analysis Questions 83

ACKNOWLEDGEMENTS

This research owes a large debt to a number of people. Special thanks are due to Howard Tumber for conducting the group discussions at very short notice throughout the country. My colleagues Steven Barnett and David Docherty acted as true colleagues in reading and helping to structure the report without complaint and intellectually in contributing to the ideas and strategy. The report is a BRU effort.

I must acknowledge the financial support of the GLC without which the project could not have been undertaken. Dr Robert Towler, Head of Research at the Independent Broadcasting Authority, was, as always, generous in his support.

I would like to express my gratitude to Stephen Tagg of the Social Statistics laboratory at the University of Strathclyde for his usual professional performance. The factor analysis could not have been done without his help.

NOP must be thanked for handling our National Opinion Survey. In particular I would like to thank Nick Moon whose support and assistance at times stretched above and beyond the call of professional duty.

Shivaun Meehan and Anna Noble typed and corrected several versions of the manuscript with their usual good natured calm.

The members of the Unit's Executive Committee are to be thanked for agreeing that such a study ought to be undertaken.

Michael Tracey, Head of the Unit, should be mentioned in dispatches. If there is a medal it is his for feeding in ideas, taking out bad ones and helping work the report into what is now I hope a readable and stimulating document.

Finally, the general public ought to be thanked. Without their answers to my questions, there would be no report. Their reward I hope will be transmitted in the more tangible form of a good future broadcasting system.

INTRODUCTION

1.1 The history of the Peacock Committee is that of an expectation by many, and an ambition of some, that a case could and would be made to make the BBC take advertising. At a stroke this would have solved 'the problem' of the licence fee and brought its form of financing more clearly into step with the dominant commercial mores of the age. We know now that such expectations were not borne out during the course of the Committee's inquiries as the signals from a battery of economic research persuaded its members that there was not enough advertisement revenue to go round and that the consequent ratings war would damage the range and quality of programmes on both the BBC and ITV. In the short term then consumerism was out. The Report however does envisage a time when de-regulation is not just possible and likely because of technological developments but a preferred means of achieving something called 'consumer sovereignty'. As such it provides a counterpoint to the collectivist, national community oriented propagation of public culture classically embodied by public service broadcasting. We shall see. This study is concerned with the wider questions of public attitudes and perceptions which have been thrown up as the debate about the future of broadcasting has moved on. For the time being the reality is that the BBC lives on through the licence fee. The original scenario of the BBC being forced to accept advertisements has given way to the possibilities of subscription and pay-per-view, both of which would have far reaching consequences for the organisation and ethos of British broadcasting, but both of which lie in the future. Structurally Peacock has settled nothing: the jury is still out.

Public Opinion Research and the Future of Broadcasting

1.2 In the past thirty years there have been in the region of twenty inquiries into broadcasting. What distinguished the latest was its direct use of survey research to consult the public about broadcasting matters, complemented by those of other interested parties (see Appendix I for list of polls). What was more, all seemed to sing the same song: the British public are overwhelmingly in favour of the BBC being made to take advertisements, if this meant reducing or removing the 'burden' of the licence fee. Attacks on the existing organisation and practices of the BBC were now apparently supported by that most powerful of instruments, the popular will. Certainly there did seem to be a remarkable unity in the poll findings and even the most ardent supporter of public service broadcasting found him or herself having to mutter that yes indeed, whatever the doubts about the wisdom of a shift in the finance of broadcasting, the people did appear to want change.

1.3 In fact it was the very uniformity and simple clarity of those market research findings which first began to trouble us. After much thought and even more research, of a rather different kind to that engaged in by the pollsters, we felt we had to engage in what Herbert Spencer once described as 'the murder of a beautiful theory by a gang of brutal facts': the simple 'truth' of the polls served to obscure, not clarify, the character and depth of public opinion. It became clear that we had been offered an illusion and had readily, if not eagerly, accepted it as a reality because like everyone else, we had simply assumed with all that cynicism which races through the veins of British life today that of course people are materialistic, of course they want a free lunch, and devil take the hindmost. Advocates and dissenters alike, those moaning, those crowing about the polls, seemed satisfied to accept that human greed was explanation enough, end of story, no further thought – at least as far as the citizenry were concerned.

1.4 The obvious solution to our doubts about the market research was to engage in our own research, through a national survey and a series of group discussions. Equally we had to examine closely the mechanics of the research undertaken by the pollsters and to speak with those responsible for the engineering of those mechanics. It became clear that the issue which had to be addressed was not just that of finance, but of what people wanted and expected from broadcasting, given the funding options which were being placed before them and which in theory at least implied differential kinds of broadcasting service. What we were after was not the topography, but the geology of the public mind. If nothing else we were saying that important cultural questions cannot be resolved by knowledge that is framed by the instrumental intellects of economists, statisticians and technocratic consultants. For example, public service broadcasting is said to imply a range and quality of programmes. What do the public *think* about such things and how does what they think affect their views on financing broadcasting? If there are other core principles which can be said to cohere to form the public service view of broadcasting what, again, does the public think, what are their judgements, and what is the equation between those judgements and those about funding? The position we were adopting was quite simple: it was that thoughts, views, attitudes, opinions – whatever one calls them – do not, on the whole, exist in the singular. They tend to exist as clusters, sometimes loosely, sometimes firmly bonded, sometimes consistent, sometimes contradictory, but always with a good deal of complexity. For that reason, the meaning of any particular part can only be grasped through the apprehension of contiguous thoughts/views/attitudes/opinions. The erroneous pursuit of the singular thought is sometimes called market research. The apprehension of the whole: social research.

Public Opinion and Financing Broadcasting: Television
1.5 Of course, the idea of public service broadcasting is hardly precise. Our immediate problem was to ask: what exactly are we examining by measuring public opinion? The method we used was to take what were broadly regarded as the main principles of the public service idea in British broadcasting, from the BRU booklet of the same name, and to translate those principles into researchable propositions.

2.1 In the course of that, however, we unearthed much information about the apparently simple question of public opinion on the BBC taking adverts.

2.2 Market research, in our view, had tended to separate individuals from their social context, to treat them in isolation. There would, for example, in the market research findings be none of the qualifications and arguments which would flow from a more natural discourse. For example, the response to our survey questionnaire seemed to show that 54% approved of the BBC taking advertisements if it meant reducing the licence fee (31% disapproved, 13% neither approved nor disapproved, 2% did not know). So even on the evidence of our own research, there seemed to be a popular mandate for making the BBC take advertisements.

However, what we also found was that public support for the BBC taking adverts, if that meant a reduction in the licence fee, is highly qualified. The public would for example not be happy with such arrangements if the programming subsequently offered was considered inferior to that which was previously available. Of the 54% who agreed to adverts only 29% said they would still accept them if it meant less choice of programmes [Table 1] which represents only 16% of the total audience for television. ITV viewers, however, were slightly more likely to agree to a reduction in choice than BBC1 viewers. ('ITV viewers' and 'BBC1 viewers' refer to channel loyalty, that is, the channel they most frequently watch.) Yet, as with everything in the real world, people are prepared to make trade-offs. Pleasure it would seem is negotiable: and three quarters of those wanting adverts still wanted them if it meant the range of programmes was reduced, but they had more of their favourite programmes [Table 2]. This represents 40% of the population as a whole. The heavy viewers, however, make up a higher percentage than light viewers; 78% of heavy viewers agreed to a reduction in range for more of their favourite programmes, compared to 68% of light viewers. Because they consume a lot of programmes a reduction in the range is no real hardship to their jaded palate. What people would object to is the buying of American programmes: 65% of those in favour objected to the taking of adverts if it meant more American programmes on BBC and ITV [Table 3]. Put in perspective, the 26% who agreed to that trade-off represented only 14% of the total population and it must also be noted that it was ITV that was by far the most heavily criticised, even by its own supporters, for having too many American programmes [Table 4].

2.3 In similar vein, of those who were in favour of adverts, 55% said they would *not* wish for this if it meant the closure of smaller regional television stations, and less than half would approve if some commercial radio stations were closed as a result of BBC TV taking adverts [Table 5]. It is not just television or programmes that individuals have in mind in thinking about cost, but a total broadcasting system. Therefore, when discussing if individuals would wish to restructure the financing of broadcasting by introducing adverts on the BBC it makes no analytical sense to concentrate only on the financial benefits adverts might bring.

2.4 The British audience has a highly supportive attitude to broadcasting, they almost seek to nurture it. For example, despite Channel 4's small share of the audience, half of those who agreed to adverts did not want them if as a result it meant a *reduction* in the service offered by Channel 4 [Table 6]. The results suggest that individuals value television and judge its offerings not by some immediate financial benefit, but in its relationship to the quality of their lives.

Therefore again we have to say that a single focus on advertising as a means of reducing cost to the viewer actually debases rather than enhances the debate about the future financing of broadcasting.

2.5 People are not concerned with whether or not they have adverts, though all things being equal they would prefer not to: everything being equal one would prefer ice-cream not to melt. The audience's concern is about the quality of the system and the type of service provided. This can be seen by the responses of those who claimed that they *would not* be in favour of the BBC taking adverts: of the 31% who initially disapproved of advertisements, 35% said that they would change their minds if adverts led to a *wider* choice of programmes, 38% if they led to better and more expensive programmes and 39% if they led to more of their favourite programmes [Table 7]. These are fairly consistent responses, leaving a rump of approximately only 17% of the total population stubbornly against adverts even if there were positive benefits in terms of programmes.

2.6 Opinions about advertising therefore are not fixed, they only appear so when speared by questions which allow the respondent no scope for reflection. What one in fact has, when that process of qualification and reflection has been articulated, is only a very small part of the population – approximately 15% – who are in favour of adverts *at all costs*, with a roughly similar proportion against adverts *whatever the benefits*.

2.7 The overwhelming majority of people are against the introduction of adverts solely as a means of reducing the licence fee, but equally the overwhelming majority are not against the introduction of adverts in principle. People might care about the cost, but what they care about more is the quality of the service. There is a sense, therefore, in which adverts only become a problem in relation to the effects they might have on the general character of the programmes offered. Viewed from this perspective it is not advertising but programming which is the main issue, as demonstrated by the fact that those who initially opposed adverts were more likely to change their opinion if adverts benefited programmes than they were if guarantees were given about the quality of the adverts the BBC might accept. 67% would still resist adverts even if those shown were of a 'very high quality', compared, for example, to only 56% if programmes were better as a result of taking adverts.

2.8 We are not trying to suggest here that the cost of the licence fee is of no concern to the public. In the discussion groups in particular there was general agreement that the licence fee was good value, but there were also complaints about the last increase and a strong desire not to see any further rises. One comment was: 'It's good value at £1 a week, we pay more than that for our newspapers', but most people did not have the inclination to engage in such accountancy and the general feeling was one of a slightly grudging tolerance to the fee rather than outright acceptance, well captured by a young woman from the North of England: 'It's just about good value, but not if it went up any more'. Our overall judgement, however, would be that there is still room to increase the level of the licence fee *without* triggering any massive and hostile reaction.

2.9 If advertising is an obvious way of raising money one at least needs to know something about attitudes to the adverts themselves. In terms of the effect adverts have on the enjoyment of television the audience is fairly evenly divided: 41% of the population agreed they would enjoy television more if there were no adverts, whilst 40% disagreed; the remainder were either unsure or had no opinion [Table 8]. Heavy viewers were slightly less likely than light viewers to agree that their enjoyment would increase if there were no adverts. Thus, at least one can say that exposure to adverts does not lead to displeasure: displeasure is based on other factors.

2.10 Although just over half the population considered there were too many adverts on TV there was no difference in agreement between light, medium, or heavy viewers as to the amount [Table 9]. What is interesting, however, is that although in general adverts tended to infringe on the pleasure of heavy viewers less than light viewers, there was no difference in agreement between heavy, medium and light viewers to the statement, 'If I am really interested in a programme I find the adverts which come in the middle spoil my enjoyment': 69% agreed that 'centre' adverts spoiled their enjoyment of a programme [Table 10]. It is also the case that 59% of heavy viewers agreed they liked 'the break adverts give between the programmes', compared to only 42% of light viewers [Table 11]. Attitudes to adverts and TV are therefore dependent on levels of concentration and time spent watching, which are related to each other. The reaction to adverts is not therefore strictly *cultural* but *behavioural*. That is, the reason adverts did not bother heavy viewers so much is they are not as concerned as light viewers with what is on TV. And the reason they enjoyed the 'breaks' was presumably that they provided an opportunity to do the things light viewers had time to do when not watching. But once their attention was taken by a particular programme, they objected to adverts to the same degree as light viewers and did so because at those particular moments they were behaving like light viewers who, to a greater degree than heavy viewers, select only those programmes they especially wish to watch.

2.11 In grappling with the question of the balance between notions of pleasure, patterns of viewing and how this would be disrupted by advertisements, one must distinguish between the fact of 'enjoyment' and the notion of 'quality': the two are not the same. For example, whereas 41% agreed [Table 8] that they would enjoy television more if there were no adverts, only 26% agreed that 'British TV would be of a higher quality if it did not have adverts' [Table 12]. Furthermore, the difference between enjoying television with adverts and believing that without them the quality would improve is most marked between ITV and BBC1 viewers on the issue of quality. For example, 30% of BBC1 viewers agreed the *quality* of TV would improve, compared to 25% of ITV viewers, but 52% of BBC1 viewers said they would *enjoy* television more without adverts compared to a much lower proportion of ITV viewers (34%) [Table 8]. There is a greater agreement therefore about the relationship between adverts and quality than there is about deriving enjoyment by the presence of adverts. Whatever individuals

mean by quality television – and heavy, medium and light viewers shared the same sentiment about the relationship of adverts to quality – the connection is not straightforward. *Quality is more than the sum total of enjoyment derived from individual programmes*: it involves, as will be seen, an estimation of the general character of the service on offer.

2.12 What then of the question of the BBC introducing adverts to maintain the present level of the licence? 50% for example wanted some other means of funding, the most popular of which, selected by 27%, was a direct government grant [Table 13]. Only 22% wanted the BBC to cut back on its level of services in an effort to keep the licence fee at its present level [Table 14]. Yet what cannot be escaped is that the most popular *single* option, agreed to by 43% of people, was for the BBC to accept some advertising. It is a rather surprising result for as one young middle class woman from the South said: 'I think you are paying for the BBC because they don't have adverts so I don't want to pay and have adverts'. But matters are not quite as they may seem.

2.13 The figures of Table 13 can be taken in two ways, neither of which necessarily contradicts the other. The fact that such a high proportion agrees to adverts to peg an already existing payment underscores our general point about adverts in themselves not being the main concern of individuals; yet the fact that the least desired option was for the licence to keep rising every few years does suggest a reluctance to part with money and a readiness to search for the cheapest option. However, as we have already seen, if it came to a choice between cheapness and the quality of the service provided, very few people would be willing to support a depletion of the programme service. What one has therefore is a concern with costs and the character of the service and, ignoring for the moment the effect on content adverts might have, a weak concern with the presence of adverts. Accepting that everything has to be paid for and that adverts are an obvious and well tried method of financing broadcasting the real question therefore is how, given the choice, would individuals negotiate their concerns when faced by the conclusion that the BBC had to accept advertising?

2.14 Only 14% opted for a form of finance in which a totally free service would be provided by the BBC being totally dependent on advertising with more advertising than on ITV at present [Table 15], about the same as the numbers prepared to accept 2 minutes of adverts per hour between 7 and 10 pm and have the licence fee rise with inflation. What is noteworthy about the respondents opting for system 1 or system 2 is that it is the heaviest viewers that go for the free service and it is the Conservatives who are the most likely to *refuse* a self-financing system for TV. For example, 21% of Conservative voters were prepared to pay an increased licence fee in line with inflation, compared to only 12% of Labour voters; and 20% of Labour voters were prepared to accept more advertising than at present on ITV if this meant no licence fee, compared to 11% of Conservative voters. Of those classified as light viewers, 20% were prepared to pay an increased licence fee rising with inflation with only a few adverts, but only 12% of heavy viewers preferred such an arrangement. Not only, therefore, are light viewers more prepared to pay directly for the service than heavy viewers, but because proportionately they consume less programmes they are in effect prepared to pay more for individual items consumed: those who at present get the best bargain are the most likely to want the free offer. It is not too surprising: the heaviest viewers are most likely to watch ITV and, as Table 15 shows, only 10% of BBC1, compared to 19% of ITV viewers, opted for the option of showing more adverts on ITV than at present. An explanation of this is the greater commitment of heavy viewers *to television* as compared to light viewers who are more selective and committed *to programmes*. Furthermore, as we have already seen, the objections to adverts were based on interruptions of favourite programmes; consequently light viewers who are likely to select only those programmes of special interest would face more annoying interruptions than heavy viewers, and thus a heavy diet of adverts was a less attractive proposition than for heavy viewers. The fact that Conservative voters are less likely than Labour voters to want a self-financing system is intriguing. Intuitively one might have thought that for them a commercial solution would be the most attractive option. In fact, what they wish to do via the licence fee is to *buy themselves out* of a culture they do not favour.

2.15 What is clear from the three remaining options is a complex trade-off between intrusion and cost. For example people would prefer to have only 4 minutes of adverts during the peak hours of 7 and 10pm, and pay the licence fee if it was held at the current level for the next five years, than to have 6 minutes of adverts during peak hours and a reduced licence fee. The fact that 21% preferred to pay the present licence fee for the next 5 years, compared to only 13% accepting a reduction but 2 minutes more of adverts, shows television is no Roman Games: the public is not to be bought by free entertainment. They will support the system to pay for the Games. The fact that the most popular option is 6 minutes of advertising per hour throughout the day, with the licence fee reduced by half, is clear demonstration of the trading of cost against intrusion: they get a reduced cost, but don't have to watch the adverts.

2.16 There is a basic tendency, when presented with options for funding the BBC by adverts, to minimise the intrusion of adverts into the system as a whole. That is, if adverts are necessary the optimum time for them is when one is not watching. However, if the BBC were to take adverts, hardly anyone wishes it to follow the pattern of the ITV system and have 'centre breaks' whereby the adverts intrude into the programmes themselves. Only 15%, for example, preferred the ITV system of adverts at the beginning, during and at the end of the programme; 77% wanted them at the beginning and end only [Table 16]. If in the future advertising is the only way to fund the BBC the public's response appears to be one of *damage limitation*.

Public Opinion and Financing Broadcasting: Radio
2.17 What then of radio? Given that radio advertising could not on its own do away with or even significantly reduce the licence fee the research simply set out to discover the level of resistance to adverts as a form of intrusion into programmes.

2.18 To the basic question, would you approve or disapprove if there was advertising on the BBC radio station they listen to most often, 35% of those who listened to BBC radio would approve, with 50% disapproving [Table 17]. Table 17 shows that Radio 3 and 4 listeners stand out as firmly against the introduction of adverts. For example, only 17% of Radio 3 and 20% of Radio 4 listeners would approve of adverts on their station. Only 3% of the radio audience selected Radio 3 as the station they most frequently listened to, and 15% selected Radio 4. 43% of the Radio 1 audience approved of advertising on their station, and 38% of the Radio 2 audience. However, although only 5% fewer Radio 2 listeners would approve of adverts than Radio 1 listeners, Radio 2 shows a 10% difference between those of its listeners who approved and those who disapproved. In comparison Radio 1 shows a mere 1% between those of its listeners who approved and those who disapproved. Thus, whatever structural arguments are advanced for Radios 1 and 2 accepting adverts, insofar as the audience is concerned Radio 1 looks the most likely candidate. That is because of the difference in audience structure between the two stations: the audience for Radio 1 is much younger than the audience for Radio 2 [Table 18].

2.19 This does not mean the young *like* adverts on radio more than the old, but that there is a difference in the way the young and the old listen to radio which makes the young less *bothered* by the presence of adverts. The young, for example, are much more likely to have the radio on as background, whereas the old are more likely to listen carefully to what is on [Table 19]. In other words, although practically the same proportion of listeners were against having adverts on Radio 1 as were for them, Radio 1 is the most acceptable for adverts because its audience in effect will not be listening to them. It is likely that they mentally switch off with the appearance of adverts and re-enter the programme when the adverts are over. It is not so much the content of radio therefore that makes one station more acceptable to adverts than another, but the manner in which the station is used.

2.20 Of those who listened to independent local radio, 34% claimed they would disapprove, and 30% that they would approve, if there were no adverts. Only 12% of the radio-listening population claimed they liked radio adverts. The apparently curious finding about those who would miss adverts on ILR seems to have something to do with the local nature of the stations which alters appreciation of adverts. For example, whereas 40% of the population claimed that what they liked about adverts on television was their amusing or funny nature [Table 20] only 6% claimed this as their reason for liking radio adverts. The highest factor of appreciation for radio adverts, given by 19% of respondents, was 'information about products and events'. This was also given by 24% of people for appreciating television adverts, but it is the comparative difference between the scores 'funny/amusing' and 'information' that is important: local radio advertising is much more functional than national advertising.

2.21 It is difficult to compare the responses to questions relating to adverts on independent local radio with the responses to the questions relating to BBC local radio accepting adverts. On the one hand one has questions about the absence of something and on the other, questions about the presence of something. On the surface it would appear that BBC local radio listeners are marginally more prepared than listeners of independent stations to have adverts. 37% of BBC local radio listeners said they approve of adverts, compared to 34% of independent local radio listeners who said they would disapprove if there were no adverts. Yet as a *group*, resistance amongst BBC listeners appears to be higher, and given the difficulty of comparing responses to two slightly different questions, it is the internal group responses that are the most interesting.

2.22 As a group, 50% of BBC listeners would object to adverts – ie when 'don't knows' are excluded more disapproved than approved. That is not the case for independent local radio listeners where more, rather than less, wished for the retention of adverts – although 36% said they did not know. Thus, whereas locality possibly gives adverts on radio a greater attraction than might otherwise be expected, locality alone cannot guarantee that advertising will be welcomed. It may be that programme content apart, people listen to BBC local radio precisely because it has no adverts. If that is the case, it would seem surprising that such a high proportion admitted they would approve of adverts. It is tempting to consider that the question of adverts is at least an open one. Certainly there is greater approval amongst Radio 1 listeners for adverts than amongst any of the listeners to other stations, but the proportion disapproving of adverts is the same as for local radio; the opinions of Radio 1 listeners, taken on the evidence of the number of 'don't knows', appears to be more fixed. On balance, therefore, when the evidence from independent local radio is taken into account, it is local radio and not Radio 1 that is the most appropriate for the introduction of adverts.

2.23 What was clear from the research is that there is a great deal of concern over the future of radio. Even though television has overtaken radio for entertainment, 61% of the population still listen to radio seven days a week: only 13% never listen at all. Radio remains a massively popular medium and is considered by most people to be either 'very' or 'fairly important' to them.

2.24 Excluding the 13% who never listen, 73% of the audience claimed radio was important to them, which is slightly more than those claiming television to be important to them. The oldest age group were much more likely to consider radio more important than the youngest age group, though in both groups there was considerable support. For example, 77% of over 55s said radio was important to them, compared to 66% of the under 25s. This should not, however, be taken as a loose attachment to radio by the young which might then make their preferred station (Radio 1) more acceptable for adverts. The old, for example, were also more likely than the young to consider television important [Table 21]. This estimation of the importance of radio to the old is as much a statement about the structure of their lives as it is about their evaluation of the service provided. Tables 21 and 22 demonstrate that the percentage of the elderly claiming television and radio to be important is the same, whereas for the young the percentage drops for radio. For the elderly, therefore, radio is important not just because of an appreciation for its programmes, but because of the place which the media in general occupy in their lives.

2.25 Given the high level of appreciation for radio generally throughout the population why should it be accepted that some stations are more ready vehicles for adverts than others? Because someone enjoys popular music does not necessarily mean they like to listen to adverts any more than someone who enjoys classical music: dissimilarities in musical taste do not make for dissimilarities in the appreciation of adverts. Structurally, the intrusion of adverts would break up the composition of Wagner more than Wham; in fact, the very structure of popular music means adverts do not have to interfere with any individual piece of music, but they do interfere with the structure of the show. Thus, whilst adverts on Radio 1 may not destroy the music as such, they may still interfere with pleasure; to give over Radio 1 to adverts but not Radio 3 could therefore be interpreted as a punishment for a particular taste in music. Surprisingly perhaps, given that the youngest age group has been raised to a greater extent than others within an advertising culture, this group is hardly more likely to approve of adverts *on BBC radio* than the oldest age group [Table 23]. In general the youngest age group are no more likely to enjoy adverts *on radio* than the older age groups [Table 24].

2.26 The real lesson to draw however is that attitudes to the introduction of advertising cannot be understood without some understanding of people's relationship to the various media. For example, adverts on television are enjoyed more than adverts on radio [Table 24]. 66% of people considered television adverts to be of a high quality, with only 8% claiming they were of low quality. The proportion believing radio adverts to be of high quality is much less at 17%, with 23% considering them of low quality. What is intriguing, however, is that despite 66% considering television adverts to be of high quality, only 40% claimed they actually enjoyed adverts on television. This underscores a very basic, perhaps even obvious, point: people do not watch television or listen to radio for the adverts, but for the programmes.

2.27 Some proof of this lies in the reasons for liking and disliking adverts on television. Although the greatest dislike, mentioned by 40% of people, was that adverts broke the continuity of programmes, when asked what they liked about adverts, 21% gave 'break to do other things'. Yet amongst the reasons for liking adverts on radio, that they provided a break to do other things was never mentioned – not surprising in the light of a comment made by one middle aged woman in the discussion groups: 'adverts on television are useful for making tea etc, whereas with radio you are invariably doing these things already'. But 23% did mention as a dislike the break in the continuity of programmes. In the discussion groups there was hostility to adverts on radio not encountered in discussions of television: 'I listen to radio four or five hours a day, but never Capital Radio because of the adverts'; 'It is more frustrating to have adverts on radio than television'; 'Adverts are more annoying on radio'; 'The only reason I listen to BBC radio is because there are no adverts'; and 'Adverts sound worse on radio – it's the jingles' were just some of the complaints. What certainly needs questioning, therefore, is the suitability of radio as a medium for adverts. Bearing in mind this question and whilst not overlooking the role that radio content might play in the acceptability of advertising, it is only by a greater understanding of the individual that conclusions can be made about which radio stations would be most acceptable to the public for commercialisation.

Market Research and Social Research
2.28 What then of the general discrepancy in the figures between our survey and most other polls on the question of advertising and the licence? In our view this was a basic function of the differential placement of those questions in the different surveys. In our survey the question of funding was number 65 whereas, for example, Gallup of November 1984, showing 66% approving adverts on BBC TV and MORI of October 1985, showing 67%, were both omnibus questions. That is, the question was placed in a questionnaire not specifically structured to discover attitudes to broadcasting, but to find out attitudes to a whole variety of issues. In Peacock's own commissioned survey, once one has ignored preliminary standard demographic questions and the establishment of listening habits, the question of willingness to allow adverts was number 4. But then there are only 17 attitude questions in all. Not only is our question on funding placed well into the questionnaire, it is immediately preceded by two questions concerning the methods of funding which would allow the BBC to keep the licence fee at its present level or

allow the continuation of the present process whereby the fee rises every few years.

2.29 Placing the questions of adverts deep into the questionnaire probably produced an awareness of issues and in some cases new ideas about broadcasting which allowed the respondent to confront the issue more reflectively than if the questions had come at the very beginning of the interview (interestingly, in the very short questionnaire administered to our groups just under 63% approved of adverts on the BBC if it meant a reduction or abolition of the licence fee – a response more in line with most opinion polls). However, although our main survey probably did have an 'educational' effect there is no reason why a survey should not educate or raise awareness. It is virtually impossible to escape such influences entirely. For example, people might not have thought about the type of bus service they wanted until asked and even if they had, might not have considered the various options presented by a questionnaire. Yet that is no reason to be suspicious of the answers or to consider they are not representative of the population as a whole: if everyone was given the questionnaire and thus exposed to the same educational influence, the sample response would turn out to be no different from the total population. What we are arguing is that statistics about attitudes to funding the BBC are meaningless if separated from a whole cluster of attitudes to the idea of public service broadcasting, and that the point of the detailed questionnaire was to examine a range of attitudes rather than just the surface of public attitudes to these questions.

Remembering Reith (1)

3.1 It might seem from the evidence of the opinion polls that the great majority of the British public is no longer committed to the BBC as an ideal or an institution. Not true. Our research unearthed if not a population of Reithians, considerable numbers of people who carry within their intellectual baggage significant elements of the ideals of broadcasting laid down in the early days of British broadcasting. Tuning into public opinion on broadcasting is like listening in to the remnants of the big bang, hissing from the edge of the known universe. What those remnants represent is the extent to which the creation of public life in the late 19th and early 20th centuries – public libraries, public welfare, public education and public service broadcasting – has entered public consciousness. For example, take the prescription that broadcasting inform, educate and entertain. All are well entrenched insofar as they relate to television: 97% of the population either agreed a great deal, or a fair amount, that it should entertain; 93% that it should inform people about what is going on in the world; and 84% that it should educate. Education might not be so firmly accepted as entertainment, but nevertheless the fact that it is so highly regarded shows an appreciation of television as more than just a source of amusement.

Cynically, the responses might be taken to mean no more than that people are against sin. What it actually suggests – and this is a view supported at various points throughout the study – is that most people's view of television is not a narrow one, but one in which television is viewed as much as a *public property* as it is a *private pleasure*.

3.2 Towards the end of their report (para 575) the Peacock Committee states: 'There seem to be as many interpretations of the concept of Public Service as contributors to the debate [about the future of broadcasting]' and go on (para 577) to say, 'We had some difficulty in obtaining an operational definition from broadcasters of public service broadcasting ....'. The BRU booklet, *The Public Service Idea in British Broadcasting*, which the Peacock quotes without comment, defines eight main principles. These are:

1 Universality: Geographic – broadcast programmes should be available to the whole population.

2 Universality of Payment – one main instrument of broadcasting should be directly funded by the corpus of users.

3 Broadcasting should be structured so as to encourage competition in good programming rather than competition for numbers.

4 Universality of Appeal – broadcast programmes should cater for all interests and tastes.

5 Broadcasting should be distanced from all vested interests, and in particular from those of the government of the day.

6 Broadcasters should recognise their special relationship to the sense of national identity and community.

7 Minorities, especially disadvantaged minorities should receive particular provision.

8 The public guidelines for broadcasting should be designed to liberate rather than restrict the programme makers.

In our research we examined public opinion on the future of broadcasting from within this framework: put simply, we examined the extent to which these propositions were shared, or not, by the general public.

3.3 *Universality: Geographic*
Only 3% of the population considered that people who live in remote areas, to which it costs relatively more to broadcast, should pay a higher licence fee [Table 25]. The principle of universal geographical provision equally shared would seem to have a good deal of public support.

3.4 *Universality of Payment.*
The majority are committed to this principle: 62% disapproved of the idea that if people only watch ITV or C4 they should not have to pay the licence fee.

3.5 *Broadcasting should be structured so as to encourage competition in good programming rather than competition for numbers*
We have already argued, and we hope demonstrated, that the majority of the public does not want advertising if it leads to a lowering in the quality of programmes and the broadcasting services as a whole. Appreciation for television goes beyond the amount and range of programmes offered, to a defence of creativity within broadcasting. Large numbers of people show an appreciation for the development and maintenance of good television, indicated by the fact that 46% of the 54% who originally agreed to advertising said they would disapprove if it led to 'less experimenting with new programmes on BBC and ITV' [Table 6].

A Question of Quality
3.6 But what do quality and creativity mean, in the context of the idea of good programmes? What, for example, is quality music or quality literature? Good of its type, or good in the sense of the best that music or literature has to offer? For most people quality simply means good – that which they enjoy. Most people do not theorize about the sorts and character of their pleasure, and most explanations of why a programme is of good quality are no more than extensions of how much they enjoyed it. Only in very vague fashion can people relate that enjoyment to an explanation as to why a programme is amusing, exciting, interesting, and so on. For example, offering the express promise, 'I'll give you a good idea of what I mean by quality' one middle aged man from a Midlands discussion group said 'Take two programmes, Sir Robin Day's *Question Time* and Anglia's *Cross Question*. I know it depends a lot on the guest speakers who are appearing on a particular night, but as far as I am concerned there is just no comparison in the presentation and professionalism of the two programmes'. Despite the man's pride and obvious satisfaction that he had indeed told us what 'quality' was, when his statement is unpicked it remains essentially vacuous. Presentation was mentioned and so was professionalism, but so also was the importance of the guest speakers. Does that mean the guest speakers had to be interesting, well turned out, articulate, have the common touch, be well known personalities, or allow Sir Robin to exercise his 'professionalism' to control the flow of the programme?

3.7 Given such difficulties we decided to make matters easier by asking in the survey what was *not* 'good quality', the assumption being that people can manage negative description more easily than positive description. This approach also has the added attraction of explaining why people watch programmes they consider to be of poor quality – the reverse, of course, requires little explanation. The other advantage is that by examining the specific programmes nominated as being of poor quality, light is thrown upon what people *associate* with quality.

3.8 38% of the population admitted to watching programmes which *they* regarded as of poor quality, spread reasonably evenly by class, age and amount of viewing. In terms of channel loyalty – the channel they watch most – both ITV and BBC1 viewers were equal and, apart from those with low commitment to public service broadcasting, no difference existed between commitment to psb and judgement of watching poor quality shows. Men, however, were more likely to watch programmes they considered of poor quality than were women [Table 26]. Although logically this might mean men are less discerning than women, the fact is that men watch shows which their partners like but which are not necessarily to their own taste. When asked why, if the programmes were of low quality, they watched them the main response of both sexes was 'someone else watching!' Thus, although individuals judged programmes in terms of quality, their basic reason for watching was their relationship not to the programme but to another person. 36% of women gave the reason as 'someone else watching' compared to 57% of men. Women were more likely than men to watch poor quality programmes from habit and for the reason of 'nothing else on'. Perhaps not surprisingly heavy viewers were more likely to watch poor quality program- mes than light viewers were for the reason of 'nothing else on' [Table 27].

3.9 Whilst the figures might suggest a male population forced to watch poor quality TV through an incompatibility of taste with that of their spouse, the sentence is a limited one: the jailer is soap opera. Men however are not the only prisoners. A frequent complaint about programmes made by women in the discussion groups was, 'Too much sport – it drives me out of the house'. Yet, whilst women might be prisoners to their husbands' tastes, or 'driven out of the house', women did not describe their reaction to sport in terms of quality, as men did for soaps, but boredom. Uninterested and possibly untutored in the various sports, quality was a meaningless concept to apply. The question of quality and soaps is, therefore, intriguing.

3.10 Coming second in overall programme popularity, soap operas are massively more popular with women than men [Table 28]. Only 18% of men placed soap operas amongst their most favourite programme types, com- pared to 48% of women. It may be, for reasons of self-identity, that men were more reluctant to admit they liked soaps than were women, but nevertheless, both sexes placed soap operas far above any other type of programme in terms of poor quality.

3.11 Mention poor quality and people think of soaps. Of those who watch programmes that they think of as poor quality 76% of men, and 73% of women cited soaps as poor quality programmes that they watched [Table 29]. It is likely that because of the frequency of such programmes the devotee of the genre has several programmes to compare, and therefore develops a critical understanding of quality (where they might not do so for documentaries on early Etruscan pottery). But the small difference between the sexes in judging soaps to be of poor quality does not contradict the overall gap in popularity of the genre: it is a product of differences between individual soap operas. One can like a programme genre, watch a particular example, consider it to be of poor quality, but still enjoy it. That is, men and women in general rank soaps highly, but differ in their appreciation of individual soaps. Asked to name the programmes of poor quality which they watch, the top four were all soaps: *Crossroads* (18%), *Coronation Street* (16%), *Dynasty* (14%) and *Dallas* (13%). Concentrating only on these, since given the sample size other programmes failed to register very high numbers, some interesting patterns emerge. The two home-spun soaps run downwards in criticism inversely to class whilst the two American imports run upwards inversely to class. Apart from *Crossroads*, men were more likely than women to cite the four as poor quality programmes which they watch, especially in the case of *Dynasty* [Table 30], and the two younger groups thought British-made soaps were of worse quality than did the two older groups.

3.12 If we move to the question of why the programmes nominated are considered to be of poor quality some insight is thrown on the above responses: 'not interesting/boring' was the main reason, but it is difficult to say what that means other than the respondents failed to like the programme.

3.13 Holding in mind that men singled out *Dynasty* in particular as being of poor quality, Table 31 is interesting because *Dynasty* scores highly for being unrealistic but *Crossroads*, which men were no more likely to rate as poor quality than women, scores the lowest for being unrealistic. It is possibly the case therefore that poor quality for men revolves more around the question of realism than it does for women. Yet one must be careful: even though Table 31 shows the reason why people consider the various soaps to be of poor quality, it is difficult to know what individuals have in mind when considering something to be unrealistic: unrealistic to life as they experience it or unrealistic as to how American oil moguls might behave? Yet however individuals determine realism the two imported soaps score the highest as being unrealistic and lack of realism was the third highest determination of poor quality. What probably rescues their popularity is that they score the lowest on poor acting, which was the second highest score for poor quality; indeed poor acting scored practically the same as the leading, but amorphous, criticism, 'Not interesting/boring'. The fact that 'badly written' is the lowest reason given for poor quality, and that the response is fairly evenly spread between the four soaps, might well mean scripting is not a judgement people bring to soaps in assessing quality. That is, it could be people simply accept that soaps are not pearls of dialogue and that the quality of soaps is judged instead in terms of character portrayal (evidenced by 'bad acting' scoring so highly in determining poor quality).

3.14 Although by no means precise, we have some idea behind the thinking people bring to the notion of quality. That poor quality was a term reserved for the entertainment end of the market, in particular soap operas, is a product of that genre's overall popularity: statistically those programmes with low viewing figures have less chance of showing as poor quality because fewer people watch them. That is one of the drawbacks of sampling. Even so it is somewhat puzzling that in examining categories of programmes [Table 29], rather than individual shows, soap operas score so highly on poor quality. After all, among light entertainment programmes chat shows have high ratings and within serious programming so does news, but only 3% and 2% respectively considered those of poor quality. Whether something is of good or poor quality would seem therefore to have something to do with narrative form: the soap opera lends itself to such judgement in a way other programmes do not. In a sense they ask to be judged by commonly agreed standards because they supposedly reflect real-life situations involving the anthropological universal of family; even if the setting is alien to the viewer, the problems of familial interaction are not.

3.15 Because quality is bounded by different meanings for different people for different programmes, and given the variety of types of programme shown on television, we would caution that, as a research question, there is a limit to the value to be gained from pursuing the general idea of quality of programmes in trying to judge what people want from TV. Furthermore, quality is not very meaningful when set within the reality of how people watch television. The comment, 'there is not much on television', is not a statement about quality, but a reference to the fact there is nothing much on of interest. Poor quality furthermore does not hinder enjoyment: one group discussant, after criticising the poor quality of *Dynasty*, said 'I know it's ridiculous, but I enjoy it'.

3.16 'Quality', in the generally accepted idea of quality as applied to say literature or music, is not the only standard people apply to television in estimating their enjoyment. It is not even the most important basis for judging television. As a check on this argument it is worth considering responses to the following question: 'Do you think it would be a good idea or a bad idea to show fewer hours of TV if the quality of what was shown improved as a result?'. On this the public was evenly divided. No patterns emerged between classes, although there is slight evidence that the heavier the viewer the more likely they were to consider it a bad idea. Of the 46% who thought it a good idea, the most popular time for reducing hours was in the morning before 12 o'clock and after midnight [Table 32]. Reducing the hours between 6pm and 8pm and between 8pm and 10pm gained only 2% and 1% support. Nobody, that is, wanted a reduction in hours during the time when they themselves watch TV. Assuming the oldest age group of 55+ retire earlier than the younger age groups an interesting check on this 'selfish factor' is that the old most approved of cutting hours after midnight. Of course it can be argued people wanted cuts at a time they did not watch so that the quality might be better at times when they did, and indeed it would be perfectly rational for them to do so. Perhaps therefore their concern was about quality, but on the evidence it seems unlikely.

3.17 What the results suggest is that in answering the question of quality, people were thinking about the quality of *the service as it affected them*. They defined quality in terms of the availability of programmes, and did not apply the notion of quality as a *critical* concept.

3.18 The question of introducing adverts, and the resistance or acceptance of them, does not revolve around just the possible effect on quality of programmes. Whilst individuals might at times apply the critical notion of quality, they have a wider understanding of television than the performance of individual programmes. Furthermore, even if quality was a prerequisite of enjoyment, something which we very much doubt, enjoyment does not mean people want more of the same. Thus to find that quality equals enjoyment would still not advance understanding of what people wanted from television.

A Question of Pleasure

3.19 By far the most popular type of programme is film, with 44% of the population nominating it amongst their three favourite programme types. The next most popular is soap opera with 34% including it amongst their favourite three, closely followed at 33% by travel and nature documentaries [Table 28]. Asked to name the actual programmes (excluding films) they enjoyed most the week before the survey, apart from the comedy drama, *Auf Wiedersehen Pet*, soap operas occupied the first eight places: *EastEnders* dominated, with 24% selecting it as one of the three most enjoyable, down to *Brookside* with 5%. Table 33 demonstrates not just the domination of soaps, but that the first two are British. Furthermore, as popular as the genre may be, the genre itself is no guarantee of individual enjoyment. Only 2% selected *The Colbys* amongst their three most enjoyable programmes and only 1% selected *Albion Market*. Many other types of programme were selected more frequently than that.

3.20 Clearly discernment exists and clearly there is something about *EastEnders* and *Dallas* which is perceived as good but which is found to be missing in the comparable soaps, *Albion Market* and *The Colbys*. One can, however, over-sud the soaps. Asked which type of programmes they would wish to see more of on TV, soaps were twelfth in the list: only 6% of the population expressed a desire for an increase in their diet of soaps [Table 34]. The appetite for films however appears insatiable, with 37% wishing for more than at present, closely followed by documentary and nature programmes. Thus any ratings battle which resulted in the off-loading of films on the public would not necessarily meet with disapproval.

3.21 Yet other factors than just straightforward enjoyment must be taken into account in gauging the public's appreciation of TV. There is a difference between *appreciation* and *enjoyment*. News and current affairs were appreciated rather than enjoyed, coming fourth in favourite types of programme. It is perhaps to be expected, but the point to underscore is that pleasure as with quality is a far from simple concept: soaps were appreciated more, and enjoyed more, than news and current affairs, but came slightly lower than news and current affairs in preferences for more programming of that type. In fact, over half the population considered there were too many soap operas on television. Any ratings war therefore, prompted by competition for commercial revenues that attempted to exploit the popularity of soaps by producing more, would lead to audience disatisfaction. We shall have more to say about this later but first it is necessary to make a comment about ratings and what they mean in terms of the production of popular culture.

3.22 Enjoyment is not preordained. What has worked as pleasure in the past may work as pleasure in the future; but it does not exclude the surprise factor and the possibility that a programme which a person felt would not be enjoyable might turn out on exposure to be agreeable and acceptable. Although only 3% claimed this *very often* happened, 20% claimed it happened fairly often, with 46% agreeing that it occurred occasionally. 30% said it rarely or never happened, but what is clear is that taste is not something that is absolutely fixed in advance [Table 35]. The fact that so many viewers were agreeably surprised suggests that for television to be enjoyed, it does not follow that it must slavishly follow ratings: the popular does not have to be what the culture critic and philosopher, Theodor Adorno, called 'the congealed results of public preference'. There seems, in fact, to be a public desire for television to depart from the routine and to experiment, even if the programmes often turn out not to be worth watching [Table 36].

A Question of Loyalty

3.23 The question is, do the public think that the present four channel system provides a framework which produces enough competition? This is prompted by Peacock's argument that if 'the right conditions are established, there will be little need for regulation apart from the general law of the land covering matters such as public decency, defamation, sedition, blasphemy and most of the other matters of concern in broadcasting' (Para 593). Peacock's reference point is publishing, but 'right conditions' looks very much like Marx's vision of the 'withering away of the state': a desired condition, but unclear as to how it is to be achieved. We can begin to see what the public feels about this by gauging their views of the different channels.

3.24 We are not overlooking the fact that at most times almost all viewers will use all four channels and it may be wrong therefore to treat the audience, as we are going to do, as BBC1, BBC2, C4 or ITV viewers.

However, despite movement between channnels, 71% of people claimed they watched one particular channel more than any other with nearly half of these claiming they watched one channel 'a lot more'. Channel loyalty, furthermore, appears remarkably stable; for example, although 15% had developed a loyalty to their particular channel within the past two years, over half of those who watched one channel more than any other had favoured the channel for ten years or more.

3.25 Despite this tendency to watch one channel more than any other, nearly half the population did not consider there was much difference between the programmes shown on BBC1 and those shown on ITV, though only 7% thought there was no difference at all between the two channels [Table 37]. What is interesting is that ITV viewers were less inclined to see a difference in the programmes shown between their channel and BBC1 than BBC1 viewers were of ITV. Those viewers most loyal to BBC2 and C4 were practically equal in agreeing with each other about the differences between BBC1 and ITV; although they were less likely than BBC1 viewers to see a difference they are closer in agreement to them than to ITV viewers. Perhaps this is not too surprising, given that they are closer in class composition to BBC1 viewers than ITV. It is reasonable to presume therefore that as much as they undervalue BBC1, compared to BBC2 and C4, they value ITV less.

3.26 The findings do present ITV viewers as standing somewhat apart from the rest in their channel judgement, but why should it be that they discerned less difference than other viewers between their channel and BBC1? More importantly, in terms of channel distinction, what is the meaning of their judgement? Do the estimations of ITV viewers hold the key to unlocking the central cultural question of the difference between a publicly funded popular channel and a popular channel funded by commercial revenues?

3.27 Given that only 43% of the population thought there was either a great deal or a fair amount of difference between ITV and BBC1, any claim that the BBC is distinctive needs to be qualified. However, ITV viewers may be less likely than any other group to see a difference because of the ease with which they can raid BBC1 for programmes similar to those which initiated their devotion to ITV. It must also be noted that ITV viewers are the heaviest consumers of television and therefore are likely to make frequent sorties to other camps to satisfy their broadcasting demands; when they do, as Table 28 shows, they will probably raid for soaps, sport, films, quizzes, series and serials. The tastes of BBC1 viewers do not allow the same reciprocal privilege as that offered to ITV viewers. It would seem likely that there is more within BBC1 to satisfy ITV viewers than there is within ITV to keep BBC1 viewers happy. One can tentatively conclude therefore that at the level of public perception BBC1 is closer to ITV than ITV is to BBC1. Added weight is given to this reasoning by examining the responses to the estimation of changes to both stations in the last twelve months.

3.28 Apart from C4, estimations of all the channels having improved over the last year were roughly the same [Table 38], with approximately 15% agreeing. C4 stands out with almost half the population agreeing it had improved. It is an interesting achievement, with the estimation shared equally between ITV and BBC1 viewers. On estimating a decline however the two channels that stand out are BBC1 and ITV. Approximately the same number considered they had deteriorated and improved, but the real interest rests in who thinks what. The numbers as a proportion of the total population are small, but nevertheless offer indications that support our argument. For example, only 9% of BBC1 viewers considered ITV to have improved in the last year, compared to 24% of ITV viewers [Table 38]. This figure may be inflated by channel loyalty, but the difference is nowhere near the same for estimations of improvement in BBC1. For example, 23% of BBC1 viewers considered BBC1 had improved, but then so did 20% of ITV viewers. There is only a 3% difference, furthermore, between the channel loyalty of ITV and BBC1 viewers in considering that BBC1 had got worse. Yet, for ITV the difference is 8%. That is, 16% of BBC1 viewers thought ITV had become worse compared to 8% of ITV viewers. This suggests that BBC1, in the minds of some, has already moved towards the taste of ITV viewers.

Remembering Reith (2)
3.29 *Universality of Appeal*
By and large the public are committed to the idea that television and radio should cater for a broad range of tastes. Although 85% of the audience claimed 'good television for me is watching my favourite type of programme' [Table 36], 94% agreed that 'good television is having a wide choice of different types of programme to watch'. Thus whilst good television for most people is watching their favourite type of programme - they like what they like to watch – it is also clear that pleasure must be set within the wider boundaries of pleasure taken from the service as a whole. Consequently to understand what people want from broadcasting it is necessary to understand how people *view* the service as a whole. But it also is quite clear from the data that there is no desire for the cheap embrace offered by advertising if this damages programmes that are already enjoyed. In order to understand what people value or how they view a programme service one needs to enquire into the values people bring to broadcasting.

3.30 *Broadcasting should be distanced from all vested interests, and in particular from those of the government of the day*
This proposition is regarded by theorists of broadcasting, and those closely involved in making programmes, as central to the justification of public service broadcasting. It is in particular central to the ideology of the BBC, hence the enormous row around *Real Lives*. The ability of a broadcasting organisation to take on controversial subjects - particularly of politics and sex – is an acid test of its commitment to public service values. The research asked: are some channels viewed as more or less likely to show 'controversial' material than others, and if so, why do people consider that to be so?

3.31 Just over half the population considered C4 to be the channel most likely to screen material involving 'bad language and explicit sex' [Table 39]. Whatever else C4 has managed to achieve in its short life such a finding is a triumph of identity. Of the two popular channels, ITV easily outstrips its competitor in the sex and bad language stakes. Only 10% of people thought BBC1 the most likely channel to include plays involving such material, compared to 22% for ITV.

3.32 If it is accepted that political satire is more sophisticated and potentially more politically disturbing than comedy shows that poke fun at members of the government, BBC2 stands out as the more contentious channel. The other three channels register practically the same scores, but with ITV considered the least likely to show political satire [Table 40]. BBC2's score might be related to the reputation of *Yes Minister*, always presuming people classify it as political satire and not comedy. 50% thought ITV the most likely channel to screen comedy which poked fun at governments. Only 17% of people believed BBC1 would be the front runner in screening that type of comedy.

3.33 What can be seen therefore is that the various channels portray different images to the public. Channel 4 is clearly viewed as most likely to enter areas that might result in moral controversy, and BBC2 the most likely to show satire. If we move away from humour and morals to political and social issues then it is BBC1 that is seen to be at the forefront in covering such issues as inner city riots, investigative programmes exposing corruption in high places and documentaries about corruption in big business [Table 41]. Curiously this is not the case when it comes to such contentious political issues as interviews with terrorists. Whilst BBC1 is a fairly clear leader in social issue areas ITV is seen as equally likely as BBC1 to include material showing interviews with, for example, members of the IRA [Table 42]. There is no difference, furthermore, in channel loyalty; each thought each other's channel as likely to include interviews with terrorists. Yet this was not the case in the area of social issues: despite their channel loyalty, ITV viewers tended to consider such matters the province of BBC1.

3.34 The public has no desire for television to be timid in the face of government. They expect it to be critical. For example, asked if during normal circumstances, when there is no national crisis, current affairs programmes should criticise government actions if they think it necessary, or avoid criticism, 75% thought they should criticise; this dropped somewhat for broadcasting during a crisis such as the Falklands war, but nevertheless at 59% there was still a substantial majority which felt that even at such moments broadcasters should be critical of governments where necessary [Table 43]. What is interesting, however, is that on this score ITV appears to serve its viewers better than BBC1. During a crisis such as the Falklands war, ITV and BBC1 viewers were equal in agreeing that current affairs should criticise the government if they felt it necessary, but during normal circumstances BBC1 viewers were more likely than ITV viewers to agree that current affairs programmes ought to be critical. When asked which channel they thought *most likely* to offer criticism of government actions, ITV came out marginally on top, with 22% considering it the most likely, compared to 18% for BBC1. It must be noted however that 36% could see no difference in the likelihood [Table 44].

3.35 When asked which channel was the *least likely* to offer criticism of government action, BBC1 topped the list with 19%, compared to only 8% for ITV [Table 45]. Neither the general public, nor its most loyal viewers believe the BBC performs any better in the area of critical reporting than commercial television. Indeed, its performance is considered to be worse, with not inconsiderable feeling that the BBC was not as independent of government as ITV.

3.36 Of those believing ITV to be the most likely to criticise, 15% gave the reason as 'independence/freedom to express their views', compared to only 1% of those who thought BBC1 the most likely to be critical [Table 46]. As interesting as this is in terms of general perception, it becomes even more interesting when considered in conjunction with the responses relating to government control. For example, 19% of those believing ITV the most likely to be critical gave as their reason 'channel not run/funded or controlled by the government', compared to only 2% of those who thought the BBC more likely to be critical. This perception of a lack of independence is given further support by the responses to the question 'which channel is less likely to be critical of the government's handling of issues?' [Table 47]. Again the highest response relates to the numbers of types of programme shown that could be expected to embody a critical element; moving to the basic question of independence, 36% who thought BBC1 to be less critical than other channels did so because the channel was held to be government run/funded/controlled or needed the government to sanction the licence fee. However, only 5% of those who thought ITV less likely to be critical did so because of its links with advertisers.

3.37 Given the number of reasons people provided for their beliefs, and that the explanations are based only on those who considered one channel more or less likely to be critical of the government's handling of issues, the numbers are not large; nevertheless they do indicate the presence of some public perception of the BBC as not free of government.

3.38 The BBC is, nevertheless, seen as more responsive to public opinion than ITV: 53%, compared to 46% for ITV, thought the BBC (BBC1 and BBC2 not separated) would take either a great deal or a fair amount of notice if it received a lot of complaints over the showing of a programme featuring terrorists [Tables 48 & 49]. When channel allegiance is examined 59% of BBC1 viewers thought the BBC would take notice, compared to 45% of ITV viewers. Indeed ITV viewers were more likely to believe BBC would take notice of complaints than would their own channel.

3.39 *Broadcasters should recognise their special relationship to the sense of national identity and community.*

This openness to criticism might appear to be to the BBC's credit, but whether it is or not largely depends on the definition of the social role of broadcasting one adopts: is it to present the nation to itself and reflect the truths the populace holds, or to operate a critical concept of truth? Whichever it ought to be, 64% of the public thought that 'television should *often* show programmes that reflect the British way of life'.

3.40 *Minorities, especially disadvantaged minorities should receive particular provision*

It is quite clear from the survey that the public do not demand a broadcasting system catering only for mass taste. For example, half of the population agree 'it is all right for television to show programmes that only a few people watch', with 35% disagreeing.

3.41 *The public guidelines for broadcasting should be designed to liberate rather than restrict the programme makers*

The phrasing of this principle is so general as to make it impossible to translate it into a single researchable question. The basic thinking behind the principle however is that broadcasting should be free to explore avenues of expression independent of interference from commercial and political pressure. While the principle may be somewhat ill-defined it is quite clear in examining the overall response of the public that most people want broadcasters to be experimental, not to pander only to ratings, to feel free to challenge government, to follow their own creativity, not to be restricted by regulations, not slavishly to follow programming formulae, or show timidity in the face of political and commercial pressure.

Multi-dimensional Man

4.1 It is only by digging below the surface of opinion that one can reach the values, displayed by the responses to the central tenets of public service broadcasting and understand general feelings and dispositions towards broadcasting. But even so one cannot get pears from an apple tree, and there is a limit to the fruit that any survey research can gather. Therefore to get closer to how people feel about public service broadcasting we conducted eighteen discussion groups throughout the country (see Appendix II). As we were looking for sets of attitudes rather than isolated opinions we asked each member of the group to express their level of agreement with a set of statements about broadcasting in general and about the BBC in particular. We factor analysed the responses to these statements and unearthed four different types of opinion about public service broadcasting and the BBC, represented by 4 types of audience which we have termed 'traditionalists', 'evaluators', 'corporation men' and 'the entertainers'. Briefly, factor analysis is a statistical technique which reduces the range of possible attitudes to a few clusters; it indicates which are the most generally held attitudes, and which are the dominant attitudes within these clusters. The benefit of this method, when combined with the results of survey research, is that it offers insight into the divergencies and subtleties which exist within the general public about the role, function and place of broadcasting in British society.

Type one: Traditionalists
This type holds to attitudes which reveal concern about the BBC's alleged extravagances, overlain by a general ambivalence about the service the BBC provides, which is held to be far too populist and downmarket.

Statements

1. It's wrong for the BBC to have breakfast television when it complains it hasn't the money to finance the existing service.

2. Adverts would make the BBC too commercial.

3. Adverts spoil the pleasure of television.

4. BBC should not be making soap operas such as EastEnders.

5. TV should concentrate on making better programmes instead of increasing the number of broadcasting hours.

6. (-) I think breakfast TV is a good idea.

7. (-) Adverts on TV are fun.

8. (-) It would be good to have more channels to watch instead of just four as at present.

4.2 As with any set of attitudes there are negative as well as positive responses. Statements six to eight of this cluster are expressions of distaste rather than approval, eg people holding this set of attitudes are strongly against breakfast television (the negative sign (-) before a statement indicates disagreement). This set of attitudes was the most common one expressed. It is essentially conservative; it expresses a great deal of satisfaction with the present four channel system, and a suspicion of the BBC taking on more commitments such as breakfast and daytime television. Interestingly, it is also extremely traditionalist, in that its anti-advertising stance is associated with a certain élitism. Advertising is associated with populist programming such as soap operas and both are firmly rejected. The massive popularity of *EastEnders* seems to contradict this attitude, and indeed in the course of discussion many people in the groups themselves rejected the idea that advertising and populist programming were connected in any way; the general trend indicated that the BBC was right to make *EastEnders* because 'it is very popular', 'it made *Coronation Street* sit up' and 'that's what people want to watch'.

4.3 People holding these 'traditionalist' attitudes would prefer the BBC to cut its costs or minimise increases by reducing some of its services rather than take advertising. In discussion the respondents expressed a desire to see the BBC compete; 'competition makes better programmes' was one comment, although it should be noted that, concerns for shift-workers apart, there was a distinct lack of enthusiasm for breakfast and daytime television. Furthermore there were many complaints about the BBC's 'extravagance' and lack of sound financial management. 'The BBC is over-staffed' was one comment; another was that 'celebrities are paid too much', supported by the example of Terry Wogan: 'He is always going on about the big spread for the guests, why do they have to be wined and dined if they get a fee?'. Other concerns were 'Steve Wright the disk-jockey flew 1st class to the US on Sunday – why?' and 'why are BBC engineers staying at 5-star hotels?'. These were not isolated comments. There was a feeling that the BBC should cut down on costs: 'I get the impression that a lot could be done to save money' was one statement, whilst another went further: 'If BBC management was better the licence would not have to go up'.

Type Two: The Evaluators
The second set of opinions lead in a similar direction to the first. Essentially it relates to people's self-image as enlightened television users; it expresses concern that there should be a diverse range of programmes on television, and that television should retain the mandate to educate and inform. By these criteria television is judged by the contribution which it makes to society as a whole. The statements with which this particular type of audience cohered were:

Statements
1. There should be a broader range of programmes on TV.

2. Current affairs programmes should always be critical of those in power.

3. TV should be more experimental.

4. I make a special effort to watch programmes that have exceptional educational or cultural value.

4.4 This cluster of attitudes in Type 2 confirms the trend that standards should be maintained even if advertising were introduced. There was also a worry expressed in the discussion groups and brought out in this factor that the range of services would be reduced. 'At the moment the BBC supports local radio and a number of orchestras, what would happen to these if the BBC was just under commercial considerations?' was the concern of one young man from the South.

Type Three: *Corporation Men*

The third set of opinions is almost a throwback to the days of the Pilkington Committee. Not only does it indicate a suspicion of ITV, it reverts to the idea that the BBC is the only television network in the world which is worth its salt. The statements here were:

Statements

1. We must protect the BBC at all costs.

2. If it weren't for the BBC British TV would be awful.

3. British TV is the best in the world.

4. The BBC has made Britain respected around the world.

5. The licence fee is good value for money.

6. ITV is more concerned about making a profit than providing a good service.

7. There should be a higher licence fee rather than advertising on BBC.

8. (-) I think it is wrong if someone can prove they never watch BBC or listen to BBC radio that they still have to pay the licence fee.

4.5 This set of attitudes expresses a positive, even proud and protectionist attitude towards the BBC as an institution. This was borne out in the discussions. 'The BBC rises to the occasion, particularly in times of crisis' was one comment. 'It's authoritative' was another. Particularly common was the view 'the BBC is recognised all over the world'.

Type Four: *The Entertainers*

Not all the types show what might be termed a disposition to public values as opposed to private satisfaction. Type 4 for example, which is concerned with entertainment and the restriction of programming range, is in some ways the opposite of 'the evaluators'. The statements here were:

Statements

1. I don't like serious programmes.

2. Panorama is boring.

3. I'd be lost without TV.

4. (-) There are too many imported American programmes on TV.

4.6 Women more than men have a tendency to articulate these attitudes. Those who hold these views have a strong attachment to television, but that attachment is focussed upon the *place* television has in their lives: it is not seen as part of the wider cultural vista of public service broadcasting. On the other hand, according to the national survey those with a high commitment to public service broadcasting thought that there were too many American imports on ITV.

4.7 The difference between 'the entertainer' and 'the evaluator' is that the former position is based on a narrow interpretation of expectations no broader than the self, whereas the latter involves a definition where to maximise one's own interest others must be included: it is both altruistic *and* selfish. That is, this type of audience does not wish to deny others (community) what they want and is prepared to make a contribution to the satisfaction of the community's wants/needs, but allied with this attitude is a realisation that to obtain self-satisfaction there is a need to subsidise other people's rubbish.

4.8 Both value positions were expressed during the course of the group discussions: statements such as 'TV is for entertainment, so as it is a leisure activity people should be able to opt out (of the fee)', and 'why doesn't everybody have to pay road tax?' exemplify 'the entertainers' whereas 'the evaluators' made statements such as, 'people who don't have children still have to pay for education', and 'we all pay rates for services we don't necessarily use'.

4.9 People who view broadcasting evaluatively – that is, evaluating it in terms of a general provision to the community – express sentiments commensurate with the ideals of public service broadcasting; those who value only what they consume, do not. Those of course are ideal types, not empirical realities. Real people do not exhibit such neatness of attitudes, they merely approximate them.

4.10 What the factor analysis demonstrates is the existence of different theoretical types who collectively make up the audience. The major question is: how common are these types, or more accurately, how prevalent are the attitudes associated with them? For that one must refer back to the survey research, which we do in our conclusion, but first it is worth making a comment on the types labelled entertainers and evaluators since in many ways they hold the key to the difference between our results and the pollsters' and capture the essence of the debate surrounding the future of broadcasting.

4.11 If most people were committed to the attitudes of Type 4 – 'the entertainers' – then the future of broadcasting could be left to straightforward market forces with hardly any supervisory body to control output. They would embrace the vision of broadcasting under the aegis of consumer sovereignty. They might complain if the results did not provide the type of entertainment they enjoyed, but the outcry would have none of the righteousness to be expected from type 2 – 'the evaluators' there would be no appeal to values wider than their own estimations of what is enjoyable. Yet, and here we come to research approaches and research values, the type of one dimensional question favoured by market researchers on for example how much the public is prepared to pay, or how they wish to pay for broadcasting is only strictly relevant to 'the entertainers'. For the rest of the population such questioning is a disenfranchisement of the mind. The pertinent question therefore is how prevalent is the entertainer type; not just for the sake of planning the future of broadcasting, but in judging the meaning of research findings about public attitudes to broadcasting.

CONCLUSION

5.1 To suggest that the majority of the British public wishes to have advertising on the BBC in order to reduce or freeze the licence fee is both to misunderstand their views on this particular issue, and to ignore their more general but none the less important commitments to public culture and public service values. In a sentence, that is the conclusion of this study. At its simplest, for example, while the opinion polls were portraying the public as predominantly consumerist, in fact 64% agree with the statement that 'poor people shouldn't have to pay the full licence fee'. What this evinces is not so much the presence of public service values, but strong civic values. Individuals do not necessarily operate from a narrow self-interested perspective. It may be that such values do not extend to other areas of social life, we do not know, but the image of the viewer being unable to see much beyond the cost of the groceries is an incorrect basis from which to debate public service broadcasting. Broadcasting for most people is seen in terms of its social value and not just as some financial deal.

5.2 We said at the beginning of our report that we were troubled by the uniformity of the results emanating from the various market research agencies showing the public overwhelmingly in favour of the BBC accepting adverts to reduce the cost of the licence. It would seem from our findings that the public is not disposed to accept the free meal. What the pollsters discovered therefore was not the audience as such, but a section of thought within that audience exemplified by what we have called 'the entertainers'. While 'the entertainer' undoubtedly exists in all of us the mistake was to conclude that this single element formed the total person. Not surprisingly given their market frame of reference, and not unreasonably since all research is infused with theory, questions constructed were of relevance only to that specific aspect of the audience, leaving no room for the other types of thought.

Curiously, the opinion pollsters rediscovered one-dimensional man. We are not denying that 'the entertainer' exists and wishes the BBC to accept advertising to keep down costs. We *are* saying that other kinds of public exist, that the polls either missed or understated their views, that they are predominant and possess a clear and powerful commitment to public service values. For example:

1) There is not the slightest evidence that the majority of the public wish the BBC to accept advertising to reduce the cost of the licence. Whether people are prepared to accept adverts has nothing to do with money, but the type of service provided. For example, only 16% of the total audience for television was prepared to have adverts if by doing so it meant less choice of programmes on BBC and ITV.

2) Not only do the public not place the cost of the licence at the front of their concern in judging television, they also view radio as an integral part of broadcasting, and would not approve of the reduced cost offered by adverts if it meant the closure of some commercial radio stations. Only about half of those who agreed initially to advertising on the BBC claimed they would still be in favour if it led to such closure, which represents no more than one quarter of the total population.

3) If there was no choice and the BBC was forced to accept advertising the public's response, in line with the above findings, would be that of damage limitation. Of the five options presented for funding by adverts only 14% of people selected the one offering no licence fee with the cost replaced totally by revenue from advertising. However, in the event of the BBC taking adverts only 15% favoured the ITV system of centre breaks – 77% of the population wanted them placed only at the beginning and end of programmes.

4) Television is more than just a source of amusement: 93% agreed that it should inform, and 84% that it should educate.

5) Because television is viewed as more than just a medium of entertainment the audience wish it to be independent of government influence: 75% believed current affairs programmes should criticise the government of the day if it were felt necessary, and 59% believed it should do so even at times of national crisis such as the Falklands war. Such attitudes demonstrate a seriousness about the role of television which could not be expected to be captured by questions focussing only on the question of the cost of the service.

6) Although people like to watch programmes they like, their concept of broadcasting is not based on the numerical popularity of individual programmes: only 35% of people disagreed with the statement, 'it is all right for television to show programmes that only a few people watch'. Nor would it appear that individually unpopular programmes should give way to more popular programmes. Asked whether a programme 'if very well made but watched by very few people should be replaced by something more popular' 45% of the public disagreed, while a similar number agreed. Large sections of the audience do have high regard therefore for 'quality' programming. Quality, however, is a difficult notion to apply, but the audience does wish

television to be imaginative. 65% agreed that television ought to be experimental even if the programmes turn out to be not worth watching. If this is translated into a cost question then of the 54% who initially agreed to adverts on BBC television as a means of reducing the licence fee nearly half would not do so if it led to 'less experimentation with new programmes on BBC and ITV'.

7) Finally, without repeating the detailed testing of the eight principles of public service broadcasting, it is quite clear from the evidence of the commitment to the 'ideals', and from the values people hold, that to move into a deregulated system for broadcasting would not be in accordance with the public will, if such a move implied a diminution or undermining of those 'ideals' and 'values'. Whatever the institutional arrangements which might be made for television and radio the public would seem to be demanding that public service values be sustained: how it is financed is important, but secondary. To have suggested otherwise in market research polls, or to deny such aspiration in the future, would be to deny or make invisible the demand and ambitions of large numbers of citizens.

TABLES

The figures in some of the tables to be presented do not always add up to a hundred. This is due to statistical weighting and at times when the total is much greater than a hundred because some questions allowed for more than one answer.

TABLE 1

Q. WOULD YOU WANT BBC TELEVISION TO TAKE ADVERTISEMENTS IF THIS MEANT: LESS CHOICE OF PROGRAMMES?

Universe: All with television
Base: All who approve of taking advertising to reduce the licence fee

	TOTAL	BBC1	BBC2	ITV	CHANNEL 4	NONE
				CHANNEL LOYALTY		
UNWEIGHTED TOTAL	558	106	13	276	16	147
WEIGHTED TOTAL	558	105	14	277	15	148
YES	164	28	2	94	2	37
	29.%	27.%	15.%	34.%	14.%	25.%
NO	344	69	10	163	9	92
	62.%	66.%	77.%	59.%	64.%	62.%
DON'T KNOW	50	7	1	20	3	19
	9.%	7.%	8.%	7.%	21.%	13.%

TABLE 2

Q. WOULD YOU WANT BBC TELEVISION TO TAKE ADVERTISEMENTS IF THIS MEANT: MORE OF YOUR FAVOURITE TYPE OF PROGRAMME BUT A SMALLER RANGE OF OTHER PROGRAMMES?

Base: All with television
Universe: All who approve of taking advertising to reduce the licence fee

	TOTAL	HEAVY	MEDIUM	LIGHT
			TV VIEWING	
UNWEIGHTED TOTAL	558	238	191	129
WEIGHTED TOTAL	558	242	190	126
YES	415	190	140	85
	74.%	78.%	73.%	68.%
NO	109	36	40	34
	20.%	15.%	21.%	27.%
DON'T KNOW	35	17	10	7
	6.%	7.%	6.%	6.%

TABLE 3

Q. WOULD YOU WANT BBC TELEVISION TO TAKE ADVERTISEMENTS IF THIS MEANT: MORE AMERICAN PROGRAMMES ON BBC & ITV?

Universe: All with television
Base: All who approve of taking advertising to reduce the licence fee

	TOTAL TV OWNERS
UNWEIGHTED TOTAL	558
WEIGHTED TOTAL	558
YES	145
	26.%
NO	365
	65.%
DON'T KNOW	48
	9.%

TABLE 4

Q: WHICH CHANNELS, IF ANY, DO YOU PERSONALLY THINK EACH CRITICISM APPLIES TO?

UNIVERSE: All with television
BASE: All

	TOTAL	CHANNEL LOYALTY				
		BBC1	BBC2	ITV	CHANNEL 4	NONE
UNWEIGHTED TOTAL	1034	278	40	390	28	298
WEIGHTED TOTAL	1036	276	41	397	25	297
TOO MANY AMERICAN PROGRAMMES						
BBC 1	304	97	13	110	9	76
	29.%	35.%	31.%	28.%	38.%	25.%
BBC 2	24	5	-	12	-	7
	2.%	2.%	-	3.%	-	2.%
ITV	434	143	26	137	13	115
	42.%	52.%	64.%	35.%	50.%	39.%
CHANNEL 4	99	29	3	40	1	25
	10.%	11.%	8.%	10.%	4.%	8.%
NONE	147	15	1	71	6	54
	14.%	5.%	3.%	18.%	25.%	18.%
ALL	87	19	7	30	-	30
	8.%	7.%	18.%	8.%	-	10.%
DON'T KNOW	101	23	2	38	2	36
	10.%	8.%	5.%	10.%	8.%	12.%

TABLE 5

Q. WOULD YOU WANT BBC TELEVISION TO TAKE ADVERTISEMENTS IF THIS MEANT: CLOSING DOWN SOME COMMERCIAL RADIO STATIONS?

Universe: All with television
Base: All who approve of taking advertising to reduce the licence fee

	TOTAL
UNWEIGHTED TOTAL	558
WEIGHTED TOTAL	558
YES	254
	45.%
NO	227
	41.%
DON'T KNOW	78
	14.%

Q. WOULD YOU WANT BBC TELEVISION TO TAKE ADVERTISEMENTS IF THIS MEANT: CLOSING DOWN SOME OF THE SMALLER REGIONAL TELEVISION STATIONS?

Universe: All with television
Base: All who approve of taking advertising to reduce the licence fee

	TOTAL
UNWEIGHTED TOTAL	558
WEIGHTED TOTAL	558
YES	183
	33.%
NO	304
	55.%
DON'T KNOW	71
	13.%

TABLE 6

Q. WOULD YOU WANT BBC TELEVISION TO TAKE ADVERTISEMENTS IF THIS MEANT: LESS EXPERIMENTING WITH NEW PROGRAMMES ON BBC AND ITV?

Universe: All with television
Base: All who approve of taking advertising to reduce the licence fee

	TOTAL
UNWEIGHTED TOTAL	558
WEIGHTED TOTAL	558
YES	245
	44.%
NO	256
	46.%
DON'T KNOW	58
	10.%

Q. WOULD YOU WANT BBC TELEVISION TO TAKE ADVERTISEMENTS IF THIS MEANT: BADLY AFFECTING CHANNEL 4 SO THAT IT OFFERED A REDUCED SERVICE?

Universe: All with television
Base: All who approve of taking advertising to reduce the licence fee

	TOTAL
UNWEIGHTED TOTAL	558
WEIGHTED TOTAL	558
YES	214
	38.%
NO	272
	49.%
DON'T KNOW	72
	13.%

TABLE 7

Q. WOULD YOU STILL BE AGAINST BBC TELEVISION TAKING ADVERTISEMENTS IF BY TAKING ADVERTISEMENTS BBC TELEVISION WOULD HAVE: A WIDER CHOICE OF TYPES OF PROGRAMME?

Universe: All with television
Base: All who disapprove of taking advertising to reduce the licence fee

	TOTAL
UNWEIGHTED TOTAL	320
WEIGHTED TOTAL	320
YES	188
	59.%
NO	113
	35.%
DON'T KNOW	19
	6.%

Q. WOULD YOU STILL BE AGAINST BBC TELEVISION TAKING ADVERTISEMENTS IF BY TAKING ADVERTISEMENTS BBC TELEVISION WOULD HAVE: BETTER AND MORE EXPENSIVE PROGRAMMES?

	TOTAL
UNWEIGHTED TOTAL	320
WEIGHTED TOTAL	320
YES	179
	56.%
NO	122
	38.%
DON'T KNOW	19
	6.%

Q. WOULD YOU STILL BE AGAINST BBC TELEVISION TAKING ADVERTISEMENTS IF BY TAKING ADVERTISEMENTS BBC TELEVISION WOULD HAVE: MORE OF YOUR FAVOURITE TYPE OF PROGRAMMES?

	TOTAL
UNWEIGHTED TOTAL	320
WEIGHTED TOTAL	320
YES	183
	57.%
NO	124
	39.%
DON'T KNOW	14
	4.%

TABLE 8

Q. DEGREE OF AGREEMENT WITH STATEMENT: I WOULD ENJOY TELEVISION MORE IF THERE WERE NO ADVERTISEMENTS

Universe: All with television
Base: All

	TOTAL	TV VIEWING			CHANNEL LOYALTY				
		HEAVY	MEDIUM	LIGHT	BBC1	BBC2	ITV	CH 4	NONE
UNWEIGHTED TOTAL	1034	356	355	323	278	40	390	28	298
WEIGHTED TOTAL	1036	364	353	319	276	41	397	25	297
DEFINITELY AGREE	173	56	63	55	66	14	49	3	41
	17.%	15.%	18.%	17.%	24.%	33.%	12.%	13.%	14.%
TEND TO AGREE	250	82	81	87	77	14	86	6	67
	24.%	22.%	23.%	27.%	28.%	33.%	22.%	25.%	23.%
NEITHER/NOR	174	59	55	61	59	4	51	3	57
	17.%	16.%	15.%	19.%	21.%	10.%	13.%	13.%	19.%
TEND TO DISAGREE	314	125	103	86	48	7	152	8	98
	30.%	34.%	29.%	27.%	17.%	18.%	38.%	33.%	33.%
DEFINITELY DISAGREE	104	40	40	24	20	2	52	4	25
	10.%	11.%	11.%	8.%	7.%	5.%	13.%	17.%	8.%
DON'T KNOW	21	3	12	6	6	-	5	-	9
	2.%	1.%	3.%	2.%	2.%	-	1.%	-	3.%

TABLE 9

Q. DEGREE OF AGREEMENT WITH STATEMENT: THERE ARE TOO MANY
ADVERTISEMENTS ON TELEVISION.

	TOTAL	TV VIEWING		
		HEAVY	MEDIUM	LIGHT
UNWEIGHTED TOTAL	1034	356	355	323
WEIGHTED TOTAL	1036	364	353	319
DEFINITELY AGREE	193	65	70	58
	19.%	18.%	20.%	18.%
TEND TO AGREE	367	136	118	113
	35.%	37.%	33.%	36.%
NEITHER/NOR	165	41	52	71
	16.%	11.%	15.%	22.%
TEND TO DISAGREE	238	104	83	51
	23.%	29.%	24.%	16.%
DEFINITELY DISAGREE	56	15	22	19
	5.%	4.%	6.%	6.%
DON'T KNOW	17	3	7	6
	2.%	1.%	2.%	2.%

TABLE 10

Q. DEGREE OF AGREEMENT WITH STATEMENT: IF I AM REALLY INTERESTED
IN A PROGRAMME I FIND THAT THE ADVERTS WHICH COME IN THE MIDDLE
SPOIL MY ENJOYMENT.

Universe: All with television
Base: All

	TOTAL	TV VIEWING		
		HEAVY	MEDIUM	LIGHT
UNWEIGHTED TOTAL	1034	356	355	323
WEIGHTED TOTAL	1036	364	353	319
DEFINITELY AGREE	347	123	123	102
	34.%	34.%	35.%	32.%
TEND TO AGREE	363	127	121	115
	35.%	35.%	34.%	36.%
NEITHER/NOR	80	30	19	30
	8.%	8.%	5.%	10.%
TEND TO DISAGREE	178	64	61	54
	17.%	18.%	17.%	17.%
DEFINITELY DISAGREE	51	18	22	12
	5.%	5.%	6.%	4.%
DON'T KNOW	16	2	7	6
	2.%	1.%	2.%	2.%

TABLE 11

Q. DEGREE OF AGREEMENT WITH STATEMENT: I LIKE THE BREAK THAT ADVERTS GIVE ME BETWEEN THE PROGRAMMES.

Universe: All with television
Base: All

		TV VIEWING		
	TOTAL	HEAVY	MEDIUM	LIGHT
UNWEIGHTED TOTAL	1034	356	355	323
WEIGHTED TOTAL	1036	364	353	319
DEFINITELY AGREE	126	57	39	30
	12.%	16.%	11.%	10.%
TEND TO AGREE	383	156	125	102
	37.%	43.%	35.%	32.%
NEITHER/NOR	175	45	64	66
	17.%	12.%	18.%	21.%
TEND TO DISAGREE	218	68	75	76
	21.%	19.%	21.%	24.%
DEFINITELY DISAGREE	110	36	38	37
	11.%	10.%	11.%	12.%
DON'T KNOW	23	2	13	8
	2.%	1.%	4.%	3.%

TABLE 12

Q. DEGREE OF AGREEMENT WITH STATEMENT: BRITISH TELEVISION WOULD BE OF HIGHER QUALITY IF IT DID NOT HAVE THE ADVERTS

Universe: All with television
Base: All

		CHANNEL LOYALTY				
	TOTAL	BBC1	BBC2	ITV	CHANNEL 4	NONE
UNWEIGHTED TOTAL	1034	278	40	390	28	298
WEIGHTED TOTAL	1036	276	41	397	25	297
DEFINITELY AGREE	81	28	3	26	2	21
	8.%	10.%	8.%	7.%	8.%	7.%
TEND TO AGREE	185	55	6	72	4	47
	18.%	20.%	15.%	18.%	17.%	16.%
NEITHER/NOR	141	34	7	41	4	55
	14.%	12.%	18.%	10.%	17.%	18.%
TEND TO DISAGREE	395	112	15	147	5	115
	38.%	41.%	36.%	37.%	21.%	39.%
DEFINITELY DISAGREE	173	30	8	84	8	42
	17.%	11.%	21.%	21.%	33.%	14.%
DON'T KNOW	62	17	1	26	1	17
	6.%	6.%	3.%	7.%	4.%	6.%

TABLE 13

Q. AS YOU KNOW THE TELEVISION LICENCE FEE PROVIDES THE BBC WITH THE MONEY IT NEEDS FOR ITS TELEVISION AND RADIO SERVICES. WHICH OF THESE DO YOU PREFER?

Universe: All with television
Base: All

	TOTAL
UNWEIGHTED TOTAL	1034
WEIGHTED TOTAL	1036
BBC TO STAY AS IT IS & LICENCE FEE TO KEEP	112
RISING EVERY FEW YEARS	11.%
LICENCE FEE TO STAY AT PRESENT LEVEL &	280
DIRECT GOVERNMENT GRANT TO TOTAL AMOUNT	27.%
LICENCE FEE TO STAY AS IT IS & BBC TO ACCEPT	444
SOME ADVERTISING FOR EXTRA MONEY	43.%
LICENCE FEE TO STAY AS IT IS & MONEY FROM ITV	126
COMPANIES TO TOTAL AMOUNT	12.%
NONE OF THESE	40
	4.%
DON'T KNOW	34
	3.%

TABLE 14

Q. DO YOU THINK IT WOULD BE A GOOD IDEA OR A BAD IDEA FOR THE BBC TO KEEP THE LICENCE FEE AT ITS PRESENT LEVEL BY CUTTING BACK ON ITS SERVICES?

Universe: All with television
Base: All

	TOTAL
UNWEIGHTED TOTAL	1034
WEIGHTED TOTAL	1036
GOOD IDEA	230
	22.%
BAD IDEA	706
	68.%
DON'T KNOW	100
	10.%

TABLE 15

Q. IF BBC TELEVISION DID TAKE ADVERTISING WHICH OF THESE 5 SYSTEMS WOULD YOU PREFER?

Universe: All with television
Base: All

	TOTAL	VOTING			TV VIEWING			CHANNEL LOYALTY				
		CON	LAB	ALLI-ANCE	HEAVY	MEDIUM	LIGHT	BBC1	BBC2	ITV	CH 4	NONE
UNWEIGHTED TOTAL	1034	255	322	231	356	355	323	278	40	390	28	298
WEIGHTED TOTAL	1036	253	325	236	364	353	319	276	41	397	25	297
1) 2 MINS ADS/HOUR BETWEEN 7-10PM & LICENCE FEE RISING WITH INFLATION	161	54	39	37	44	52	64	57	9	33	6	56
	16.%	21.%	12.%	16.%	12.%	15.%	20.%	21.%	23.%	8.%	25.%	19.%
2) 4 MINS ADS/HOUR BETWEEN 7-10PM & LICENCE FEE AT PRESENT LEVEL FOR FIVE YEARS	220	65	59	58	65	72	83	79	12	67	5	58
	21.%	26.%	18.%	24.%	18.%	21.%	26.%	29.%	28.%	17.%	21.%	19.%
3) 6 MINS ADS/HOUR BETWEEN 7-10PM & REDUCED LICENCE FEE	139	30	42	41	56	44	39	26	7	62	4	39
	13.%	12.%	13.%	17.%	15.%	13.%	12.%	10.%	18.%	16.%	17.%	13.%
4) 6 MINS ADS/HOUR THROUGHOUT THE DAY & LICENCE FEE REDUCED BY HALF	305	71	102	66	112	125	68	68	7	142	5	83
	29.%	28.%	31.%	28.%	31.%	35.%	21.%	25.%	18.%	36.%	21.%	28.%
5) MORE ADS THAN ITV THROUGHOUT THE DAY & NO LICENCE FEE AT ALL	144	27	64	23	68	38	38	28	3	73	4	35
	14.%	11.%	20.%	10.%	19.%	11.%	12.%	10.%	8.%	19.%	17.%	12.%
DON'T KNOW	67	5	20	12	19	21	27	18	2	20	-	27
	6.%	2.%	6.%	5.%	5.%	6.%	9.%	6.%	5.%	5.%	-	9.%

44

TABLE 16

Q. IF BBC TELEVISION WERE TO TAKE ADVERTISEMENTS WHICH OF THESE TWO SYSTEMS WOULD YOU PREFER?

Universe: All with television
Base: All

	TOTAL
UNWEIGHTED TOTAL	1034
WEIGHTED TOTAL	1036
ADVERTISING AT THE BEGINNING AND END	799
BUT NOT DURING A PROGRAMME	77.%
ADVERTISING AT THE BEGINNING, DURING	160
AND END OF THE PROGRAMME AS NOW ON ITV	15.%
DON'T KNOW	78
	7.%

TABLE 17

Q. WOULD YOU APPROVE OR DISAPPROVE IF THERE WAS ADVERTISING ON BBC RADIO?

Base: All who listen to BBC radio nowadays

	RADIO STATION LISTENED TO MOST OFTEN NOWADAYS				
	TOTAL	**RADIO 1**	**RADIO 2**	**RADIO 3**	**RADIO 4**	**BBC LOCAL RADIO**
UNWEIGHTED TOTAL	618	222	157	24	141	80
WEIGHTED TOTAL	615	213	160	25	139	85
APPROVE	213	91	60	4	28	31
	35.%	43.%	38.%	17.%	20.%	37.%
DISAPPROVE	308	89	77	18	93	36
	50.%	42.%	48.%	71.%	67.%	42.%
DON'T KNOW	94	33	23	3	17	18
	15.%	15.%	14.%	13.%	12.%	21.%

TABLE 18

Q. WHICH ONE RADIO STATION DO YOU LISTEN TO MOST OFTEN NOWADAYS?

Universe: All who listen to the radio
Base: All

	TOTAL	AGE			
		UNDER 25	25-34	35-54	55+
UNWEIGHTED TOTAL	922	152	188	285	287
WEIGHTED TOTAL	920	129	192	292	301
RADIO 1	213	81	69	48	13
	23.%	63.%	36.%	17.%	4.%
RADIO 2	160	3	14	70	71
	17.%	2.%	7.%	24.%	24.%
RADIO 3	25	2	-	9	14
	3.%	2.%	-	3.%	5.%
RADIO 4	139	4	17	43	73
	15.%	3.%	9.%	15.%	24.%
BBC LOCAL RADIO	85	7	7	28	42
	9.%	6.%	4.%	10.%	14.%
BBC WORLD SERVICE	2	-	-	1	1
	*	-	-	*	*
ANY BBC STATION	615	96	107	197	211
	67.%	74.%	56.%	68.%	70.%
INDEPENDENT LOCAL RADIO	191	19	51	69	49
	21.%	15.%	27.%	24.%	16.%
PIRATE STATIONS	5	1	3	1	-
	1.%	1.%	2.%	*	-

* = less than .5

TABLE 19

Q. WHEN YOU HAVE THE RADIO ON WOULD YOU SAY THAT YOU . . . ?

Universe: All who listen to the radio
Base: All who listen to the radio

			AGE		
	TOTAL	UNDER 25	25-34	35-54	55+
UNWEIGHTED TOTAL	922	152	188	285	287
WEIGHTED TOTAL	920	129	192	292	301
ALWAYS LISTEN	215	13	25	60	115
CAREFULLY TO IT	23.%	10.%	13.%	21.%	38.%
USUALLY LISTEN	287	36	62	89	98
CAREFULLY TO IT	31.%	28.%	32.%	31.%	32.%
USUALLY JUST HAVE					
IT ON IN THE	191	34	47	68	40
BACKGROUND	21.%	26.%	25.%	23.%	13.%
ALWAYS HAVE IT					
ON IN THE	64	18	18	16	13
BACKGROUND	7.%	14.%	9.%	5.%	4.%
HALF AND HALF	160	29	39	57	35
	17.%	23.%	20.%	19.%	11.%
DON'T KNOW	4	-	1	2	1
	*	-	1.%	1.%	*

* = less than .5

TABLE 20

Q. WHAT DO YOU LIKE ABOUT HAVING ADVERTISING ON TELEVISION?

Universe: All with television
Base: All

	TOTAL
UNWEIGHTED TOTAL	1034
WEIGHTED TOTAL	1036
Total mentions:	
BREAK TO DO OTHER THINGS	216
	21.%
INFORMATION ON NEW PRODUCTS	243
	24.%
FUN TO WATCH/AMUSING	419
	40.%
OTHER	98
	9.%
NOTHING	287
	28.%
DON'T KNOW	31
	3.%

contd.

TABLE 20
contd.

Q. WHAT DO YOU LIKE ABOUT HAVING ADVERTISING ON THE RADIO?

Universe: All with television who ever listen to radio
Base: All

	TOTAL
UNWEIGHTED TOTAL	898
WEIGHTED TOTAL	898
Total mentions:	
INFORMATION ON NEW PRODUCTS/ EVENTS	171
	19.%
FUN/AMUSING	51
	6.%
OTHER	48
	5.%
NOTHING	543
	60.%
DON'T KNOW	112
	13.%

TABLE 21

Q. OVERALL HOW IMPORTANT WOULD YOU SAY THE RADIO IS TO YOU THESE DAYS?

Universe: All who listen to the radio
Base: All who listen to the radio.

			AGE		
	TOTAL	UNDER 25	25-34	35-54	55+
UNWEIGHTED TOTAL	998	152	188	285	287
WEIGHTED TOTAL	898	129	192	292	301
VERY IMPORTANT	238	15	35	71	125
	27.%	11.%	18.%	24.%	41.%
FAIRLY IMPORTANT	412	71	85	153	109
	46.%	55.%	44.%	53.%	36.%
NOT VERY IMPORTANT	228	38	67	63	61
	25.%	29.%	35.%	22.%	20.%
NOT AT ALL IMPORTANT	20	5	5	4	6
	2.%	4.%	3.%	1.%	2.%
DON'T KNOW	-	-	-	-	-
	-	-	-	-	-

TABLE 22

Q. GENERALLY SPEAKING HOW IMPORTANT TO YOU IS WATCHING TELEVISION?

Universe: All with television
Base: All

	TOTAL	AGE			
		UNDER 25	25-34	35-54	55+
UNWEIGHTED TOTAL	1034	166	202	316	346
WEIGHTED TOTAL	1036	141	206	323	362
VERY IMPORTANT	275	20	41	63	148
	27.%	14.%	20.%	19.%	41.%
FAIRLY IMPORTANT	431	60	98	141	132
	42.%	43.%	47.%	44.%	37.%
NOT VERY IMPORTANT	274	54	56	98	67
	26.%	38.%	27.%	30.%	19.%
NOT AT ALL IMPORTANT	54	7	12	21	14
	5.%	5.%	6.%	6.%	4.%
DON'T KNOW	2	-	-	1	1
	*	-	-	*	*

* = less than .5

TABLE 23

Q. WOULD YOU APPROVE OR DISAPPROVE IF THERE WAS ADVERTISING ON RADIO?

Universe: All who listen to the radio
Base: All who listen to BBC radio nowadays

	TOTAL	AGE			
		UNDER 25	25-34	35-54	55+
UNWEIGHTED TOTAL	618	107	110	194	201
WEIGHTED TOTAL	615	96	107	197	211
APPROVE	213	37	35	65	75
	35.%	38.%	32.%	33.%	35.%
DISAPPROVE	308	39	59	105	103
	50.%	41.%	55.%	53.%	49.%
DON'T KNOW	94	20	14	27	34
	15.%	21.%	13.%	14.%	16.%

TABLE 24

Q. ON THE WHOLE, HOW MUCH DO YOU LIKE OR DISLIKE HAVING ADVERTISE-
MENTS ON TELEVISION?

Universe: All with television
Base: All

		AGE			
	TOTAL	UNDER 25	25-34	35-54	55+
UNWEIGHTED TOTAL	1034	166	202	316	346
WEIGHTED TOTAL	1036	141	206	323	362
LIKE THEM A LOT	64	18	17	16	14
	6.%	13.%	8.%	5.%	4.%
LIKE THEM A LITTLE	247	40	51	75	81
	24.%	28.%	25.%	23.%	22.%
NEITHER/NOR	378	48	81	113	134
	36.%	34.%	39.%	35.%	37.%
DISLIKE THEM A LITTLE	191	28	40	57	66
	18.%	20.%	19.%	18.%	18.%
DISLIKE THEM A LOT	150	6	14	63	66
	14.%	4.%	7.%	19.%	18.%
DON'T KNOW	6	-	3	-	1
	1.%	-	2.%	-	*

Q. ON THE WHOLE, HOW MUCH DO YOU LIKE OR DISLIKE HAVING ADVERTISE-
MENTS ON RADIO?

Universe: All with television, who ever listen to radio
Base: All

		AGE			
	TOTAL	UNDER 25	25-34	35-54	55+
UNWEIGHTED TOTAL	898	150	183	280	283
WEIGHTED TOTAL	898	127	187	285	297
LIKE THEM A LOT	20	3	6	5	5
	2.%	2.%	3.%	2.%	1.%
LIKE THEM A LITTLE	86	13	22	29	22
	10.%	10.%	12.%	10.%	7.%
NEITHER/NOR	436	60	96	129	150
	48.%	47.%	51.%	45.%	51.%
DISLIKE THEM A LITTLE	145	30	29	44	41
	16.%	24.%	16.%	15.%	14.%
DISLIKE THEM A LOT	198	20	30	77	70
	22.%	16.%	16.%	27.%	24.%
DON'T KNOW	14	1	3	2	8
	2.%	1.%	2.%	1.%	3.%

TABLE 25

Q. IT COSTS MORE PER PERSON TO BROADCAST TO REMOTE AREAS OF THE
COUNTRY THAN IT DOES TO THE TOWNS AND CITIES. DO YOU THINK PEOPLE
IN REMOTE AREAS SHOULD PAY A HIGHER LICENCE FEE BECAUSE OF THIS,
OR IS IT RIGHT EVERYONE PAYS THE SAME?

Universe: All with television
Base: All

	TOTAL
UNWEIGHTED TOTAL	1034
WEIGHTED TOTAL	1036
SHOULD PAY MORE	28
	3.%
SHOULD PAY THE SAME	981
	95.%
DON'T KNOW	26
	3.%

TABLE 26

Q: ARE THERE ANY PROGRAMMES THAT YOU WATCH NOWADAYS WHICH YOU
THINK ARE OF POOR QUALITY?

Universe: All with television
Base: All

	TOTAL	SEX		TV VIEWING		
		MALE	FEMALE	HEAVY	MEDIUM	LIGHT
UNWEIGHTED TOTAL	1034	486	548	356	355	323
WEIGHTED TOTAL	1036	486	550	364	353	319
YES	391	212	179	139	135	118
	38.%	44.%	33.%	38.%	38.%	37.%
NO	636	272	364	221	216	198
	61.%	56.%	66.%	61.%	61.%	62.%
DON'T KNOW	8	2	6	4	1	3
	1.%	*	1.%	1.%	*	1.%

* = less than .5

TABLE 27

Q: WHY DO YOU WATCH THEM [POOR QUALITY PROGRAMMES]?

Universe: All with television
Base: All who watch poor quality programmes

	TOTAL	SEX		TV VIEWING		
		MALE	FEMALE	HEAVY	MEDIUM	LIGHT
UNWEIGHTED TOTAL	394	213	181	139	136	119
WEIGHTED TOTAL	391	212	179	139	135	118
NOTHING ELSE ON	87	42	45	36	29	22
	22.0%	20.0%	25.0%	26.0%	22.0%	19.0%
SOMEONE ELSE WATCHING IT/ THEM	186	122	64	55	71	60
	47.0%	57.0%	36.0%	39.0%	53.0%	51.0%
IT IS RELAXING	15	6	8	6	5	3
	4.0%	3.0%	5.0%	5.0%	4.0%	3.0%
HABIT/WATCHED FOR A LONG TIME	46	19	27	19	12	16
	12.0%	9.0%	15.0%	14.0%	9.0%	13.0%
OTHER	63	29	34	23	20	20
	16.0%	14.0%	19.0%	17.0%	15.0%	17.0%
DON'T KNOW	26	12	15	9	9	7
	7.0%	5.0%	8.0%	7.0%	7.0%	6.0%

TABLE 28

Q: USING THIS CARD PLEASE TELL ME WHICH ARE YOUR 3 FAVOURITE TYPES
OF TELEVISION PROGRAMMES.

Universe: All with television
Base: All

		SEX		CHANNEL LOYALTY				
	TOTAL	MALE	FEMALE	BBC1	BBC2	ITV	CH 4	NONE
UNWEIGHTED TOTAL	1034	486	548	278	40	390	28	298
WEIGHTED TOTAL	1036	486	550	276	41	397	25	297
FILMS	453	233	220	98	12	192	17	135
	44.%	48.%	40.%	35.%	28.%	48.%	67.%	46.%
SOAP OPERAS	352	86	266	59	2	197	4	89
	34.%	18.%	48.%	21.%	5.%	50.%	17.%	30.%
TRAVEL & NATURE DOCU-MENTARIES	341	171	170	123	24	81	6	107
	33.%	35.%	31.%	44.%	59.%	20.%	25.%	36.%
NEWS & CUR-RENT AFFAIRS PROGRAMMES	322	179	143	116	26	73	13	93
	31.%	37.%	26.%	42.%	64.%	19.%	50.%	31.%
SPORTS PROGRAMMES	284	222	62	86	12	111	4	71
	27.%	46.%	11.%	31.%	28.%	28.%	17.%	24.%
COMEDIES	267	152	114	75	1	102	7	82
	26.%	31.%	21.%	27.%	3.%	26.%	29.%	28.%
QUIZZES & PANEL GAMES	264	80	185	42	6	145	5	66
	26.%	16.%	34.%	15.%	15.%	37.%	21.%	22.%
DRAMA/PLAYS	167	56	111	57	4	54	2	50
	16.%	11.%	20.%	21.%	10.%	13.%	8.%	17.%
SERIES & SERIALS	169	52	116	37	3	89	2	38
	16.%	11.%	21.%	13.%	8.%	22.%	8.%	13.%
OTHER DOCU-MENTARIES	132	76	57	39	16	31	6	40
	13.%	16.%	10.%	14.%	38.%	8.%	25.%	13.%
SPECIAL INTEREST PROGRAMMES SUCH AS GAR-DENING OR SAILING	92	44	48	30	12	20	2	28
	9.%	9.%	9.%	11.%	28.%	5.%	8.%	10.%
CHAT SHOWS	85	20	65	18	1	38	-	28
	8.%	4.%	12.%	6.%	3.%	10.%	-	10.%

TABLE 28
Contd.

Q: USING THIS CARD PLEASE TELL ME WHICH ARE YOUR 3 FAVOURITE TYPES
OF TELEVISION PROGRAMMES?

Universe: All with television
Base: All

		SEX		CHANNEL LOYALTY				
	TOTAL	MALE	FEMALE	BBC1	BBC2	ITV	CH 4	NONE
MUSIC	79	38	41	22	2	23	6	25
	8.%	8.%	7.%	8.%	5.%	6.%	25.%	8.%
PROGRAMMES FOR CHILDREN	34	5	28	10	-	15	-	8
	3.%	1.%	5.%	4.%	-	4.%	-	3.%
ARTS PROGRAMMES	24	10	14	8	4	-	-	12
	2.%	2.%	2.%	3.%	10.%	-	-	4.%
VARIETY	27	10	17	6	-	12	-	9
	3.%	2.%	3.%	2.%	-	3.%	-	3.%
VARIETY & MUSIC	23	9	14	7	1	6	1	7
	2.%	2.%	2.%	3.%	3.%	2.%	4.%	2.%
OTHER	7	4	3	3	1	1	-	2
	1.%	1.%	1.%	1.%	3.%	*	-	1.%
DON'T KNOW	2	1	1	-	-	1	-	1
	*	*	*	-	-	*	-	*

* = less than .5

TABLE 29

Q. WHICH PROGRAMME OR PROGRAMMES ARE THESE [POOR QUALITY PROGRAMMES]?

UNIVERSE: All with television
BASE: All poor quality programmes coded at Q40

		SEX	
	TOTAL	**MALE**	**FEMALE**
UNWEIGHTED TOTAL	434	263	171
WEIGHTED TOTAL	434	266	169
NEWS & CURRENT AFFAIRS	7	5	2
	2.%	2.%	1.%
TRAVEL & NATURE	-	-	-
DOCUMENTARIES	-	-	-
OTHER DOCUMENTARIES	-	-	-
	-	-	-
FILMS	-	-	-
	-	-	-
SERIES & SERIALS	8	5	3
	2.%	2.%	2.%
SOAP OPERAS	318	198	120
	73.%	76.%	73.%
CHAT SHOWS	15	10	4
	3.%	4.%	4.%
QUIZZES & PANEL GAMES	36	21	15
	8.%	8.%	9.%
COMEDIES	18	6	12
	4.%	2.%	7.%
DRAMA/PLAYS	2	2	-
	*	1.%	-
SPECIAL INTEREST	-	-	-
CHILDRENS PROGRAMMES	1	1	-
	*	*	-
VARIETY	3	1	2
	1.%	*	1.%
MUSIC	13	8	4
	3.%	3.%	3.%
SPORT	-	-	-
OTHER	3	3	-
	1.%	1.%	-

* = less than .5

TABLE 30

Q. WHICH PROGRAMME OR PROGRAMMES ARE THESE [POOR QUALITY PROGRAMMES]?

Universe: All who watch television   Base: All who watch poor quality programmes.

	TOTAL	SEX		GROUP				AGE			
		MALE	FEMALE	AB	C1	C2	DE	UNDER 25	25-34	35-54	55+
UNWEIGHTED TOTAL	394	213	181	66	93	116	116	71	82	130	109
WEIGHTED TOTAL	391	212	179	64	91	121	112	64	81	131	113
CROSSROADS	70	39	31	4	14	29	23	15	21	18	17
	18.%	18.%	18.%	7.%	15.%	24.%	21.%	23.%	26.%	14.%	15.%
CORONATION STREET	62	40	22	7	13	22	20	16	14	17	16
	16.%	19.%	12.%	11.%	14.%	18.%	18.%	25.%	17.%	13.%	14.%
DYNASTY	57	39	18	14	13	21	9	9	9	23	15
	14.%	18.%	10.%	21.%	14.%	17.%	8.%	15.%	12.%	18.%	13.%
DALLAS	49	30	19	15	13	16	6	6	5	25	13
	13.%	14.%	11.%	23.%	14.%	13.%	6.%	10.%	6.%	19.%	13.%
PRICE IS RIGHT	24	14	10	4	7	7	5	2	5	14	3
	6.%	6.%	6.%	7.%	8.%	6.%	5.%	3.%	6.%	10.%	3.%
EASTENDERS	23	16	7	8	3	7	4	3	4	7	8
	6.%	7.%	4.%	13.%	3.%	6.%	4.%	5.%	5.%	6.%	7.%
EMMERDALE FARM	18	8	9	2	6	7	2	5	3	5	4
	5.%	4.%	5.%	3.%	7.%	6.%	2.%	8.%	4.%	4.%	4.%
TERRY WOGAN	13	9	3	1	2	8	1	2	2	5	3
	3.%	4.%	2.%	2.%	2.%	7.%	1.%	3.%	3.%	4.%	3.%
COLBYS	13	8	4	1	2	6	3	1	5	3	3
	3.%	4.%	2.%	2.%	2.%	5.%	3.%	2.%	6.%	2.%	3.%
ALBION MARKET	8	3	5	-	3	3	2	1	4	1	2
	2.%	1.%	3.%	-	3.%	3.%	2.%	2.%	5.%	1.%	2.%

TABLE 31

Q. WHY DO YOU THINK THEY ARE OF POOR QUALITY?

Base: All who watch poor quality programmes

	TOTAL	CROSS-ROADS	CORONA-TION ST	DYNASTY	DALLAS
UNWEIGHTED TOTAL	394	72	60	54	49
WEIGHTED TOTAL	391	70	62	57	49
POOR STORY-LINE	98	29	21	22	16
	25.%	42.%	34.%	39.%	32.%
BADLY WRITTEN	40	10	9	7	6
	10.%	15.%	15.%	13.%	13.%
BAD ACTING	112	42	24	21	12
	29.%	60.%	39.%	37.%	23.%
BAD PRESENTATION/	78	10	12	9	10
CHEAP	20.%	15.%	19.%	17.%	21.%
UNREALISTIC	84	16	19	24	23
	21.%	22.%	31.%	43.%	47.%
NOT INTERESTING/	116	22	16	15	12
BORING	30.%	31.%	25.%	26.%	23.%
BAD TASTE/IMMORAL/	59	6	6	8	6
HARMFUL	15.%	9.%	10.%	15.%	13.%
DISLIKE TYPE OF	45	6	4	4	3
HUMOUR	12.%	9.%	7.%	7.%	6.%
OTHER	91	9	14	9	8
	12.%	13.%	22.%	17.%	17.%
DON'T KNOW	7	-	-	-	-
	2.%	-	-	-	-

TABLE 32

Q. AT WHAT TIMES OF DAY DO YOU THINK THERE SHOULD BE FEWER HOURS
OF TELEVISION?

Universe: All with television
Base: All who think there should be fewer hours of television.

		AGE			
	TOTAL	**UNDER 25**	**25-34**	**35-54**	**55+**
UNWEIGHTED TOTAL	468	60	66	147	192
WEIGHTED TOTAL	476	52	68	151	202
6AM-10AM	259	20	36	76	128
	54.%	38.%	52.%	50.%	64.%
10AM-12AM	213	22	27	64	100
	45.%	42.%	40.%	42.%	49.%
12AM-2PM	89	7	15	34	33
	19.%	14.%	22.%	22.%	16.%
2PM-4PM	113	14	21	43	36
	24.%	26.%	31.%	28.%	18.%
4PM-6PM	40	2	3	14	21
	8.%	4.%	6.%	3.%	1.%
6PM – 8PM	12	2	4	4	1
	2.%	4.%	6.%	3.%	1.%
8PM-10PM	5	1	2	-	1
	1.%	2.%	3.%	-	1.%
10PM-12AM	38	1	2	12	22
	8.%	2.%	3.%	8.%	11.%
AFTER 12AM	162	16	18	47	79
	34.%	30.%	26.%	31.%	39.%
DON'T KNOW	9	1	1	5	2
	2.%	2.%	2.%	3.%	1.%

TABLE 33

Q: WOULD YOU NAME THE THREE PROGRAMMES YOU ENJOYED MOST ON TELEVISION LAST WEEK?

Universe: All with television
Base: All

	TOTAL
UNWEIGHTED TOTAL	1034
WEIGHTED TOTAL	1036
EASTENDERS	252
	24.0%
CORONATION STREET	167
	16.0%
DALLAS	145
	14.0%
EMMERDALE FARM	87
	8.0%
AUF WIEDERSEHEN PET	73
	7.0%
DYNASTY	65
	6.0%
CROSSROADS	67
	6.0%
BROOKSIDE	52
	5.0%
TERRY WOGAN	47
	5.0%
NEWS (UNSP)	44
	4.0%

For reasons of space only the first 10 highest scores out of a total of 64 programmes mentioned.

TABLE 34

Q: WHICH OF THESE TYPES OF PROGRAMME WOULD YOU LIKE TO SEE MORE
OF ON THE TELEVISION?

Universe: All with television
Base: All

	TOTAL
UNWEIGHTED TOTAL	1034
WEIGHTED TOTAL	1036
FILMS	388
	37.%
TRAVEL & NATURE DOCUMENTARIES	324
	31.%
DRAMA/PLAYS	229
	22.%
COMEDIES	195
	19.%
OTHER DOCUMENTARIES	185
	18.%
MUSIC	150
	14.%
SERIES & SERIALS	142
	14.%
SPORTS PROGRAMMES	139
	13.%
SPECIAL INTEREST PROGRAMMES SUCH AS GARDENING OR SAILING	135
	13.%
QUIZZES & PANEL GAMES	127
	12.%
NEWS & CURRENT AFFAIRS PROGRAMMES	90
	9.%
SOAP OPERAS	60
	6.%
CHAT SHOWS	60
	6.%
VARIETY	60
	6.%
PROGRAMMES FOR CHILDREN	57
	5.%
ARTS PROGRAMMES	44
	4.%
VARIETY & MUSIC	22
	2.%
OTHER	38
	4.%
DON'T KNOW	54
	5.%

TABLE 35

Q: HOW OFTEN IF AT ALL DO YOU PUT ON PROGRAMMES THAT YOU DON'T THINK YOU WILL LIKE AND THEN FIND THAT YOU ACTUALLY ENJOY THEM?

Universe: All with television
Base: All

		TV VIEWING		
	TOTAL	**HEAVY**	**MEDIUM**	**LIGHT**
UNWEIGHTED TOTAL	1034	356	355	323
WEIGHTED TOTAL	1036	364	353	319
VERY OFTEN	33	18	10	4
	3.0%	5.0%	3.0%	1.0%
FAIRLY OFTEN	207	91	77	39
	20.0%	25.0%	22.0%	12.0%
OCCASIONALLY	473	165	147	162
	46.0%	45.0%	42.0%	51.0%
RARELY	246	73	89	83
	24.0%	20.0%	25.0%	26.0%
NEVER	64	15	21	28
	6.0%	4.0%	6.0%	9.0%
DON'T KNOW	14	2	8	3
	1.0%	1.0%	2.0%	1.0%

TABLE 36

Q. TELEVISION PROGRAMMERS SHOULD TRY AND EXPERIMENT EVEN IF THE PROGRAMMES OFTEN TURN OUT NOT TO BE WORTH WATCHING.

Universe: All with television
Base: All

	TOTAL
UNWEIGHTED TOTAL	1034
WEIGHTED TOTAL	1036
DEFINITELY AGREE	149
	14.0%
TEND TO AGREE	524
	51.0%
NEITHER	107
	10.0%
TEND TO DISAGREE	165
	16.0%
DEFINITELY DISAGREE	61
	6.0%
DON'T KNOW	30
	3.0%

contd.

TABLE 36
contd.

Q: DEGREE OF AGREEMENT WITH STATEMENT: GOOD TELEVISION FOR ME IS WATCHING MY FAVOURITE TYPE OF PROGRAMME.

DEFINITELY AGREE	468
	45.0%
TEND TO AGREE	416
	40.0%
NEITHER	56
	5.0%
TEND TO DISAGREE	79
	8.0%
DEFINITELY DISAGREE	9
	1.0%
DON'T KNOW	8
	1.0%

TABLE 37

Q: APART FROM THE ADVERTISEMENTS HOW MUCH DIFFERENCE DO YOU THINK THERE IS BETWEEN THE PROGRAMMES ON BBC1 AND ITV?

Universe: All with television
Base: All

	TOTAL	GROUP				CHANNEL LOYALTY				
		AB	C1	C2	DE	BBC1	BBC2	ITV	CH 4	NONE
UNWEIGHTED TOTAL	1034	173	236	283	338	278	40	390	28	298
WEIGHTED TOTAL	1036	170	233	295	334	276	41	397	25	297
A GREAT DEAL	136	33	26	34	43	49	9	57	3	18
	13.%	19.%	11.%	11.%	13.%	18.%	23.%	14.%	13.%	6.%
A FAIR AMOUNT	310	54	86	80	90	110	13	113	9	64
	30.%	31.%	37.%	27.%	27.%	40.%	31.%	29.%	38.%	22.%
NOT VERY MUCH	476	70	100	149	155	97	16	193	10	161
	46.%	41.%	43.%	51.%	47.%	35.%	38.%	49.%	42.%	54.%
NONE AT ALL	78	8	15	27	26	10	1	23	2	41
	7.%	5.%	6.%	9.%	8.%	4.%	3.%	6.%	8.%	14.%
DON'T KNOW	36	5	6	5	19	9	2	10	-	14
	3.%	3.%	3.%	2.%	6.%	3.%	5.%	3.%	-	5.%

TABLE 38

Q. OVER THE LAST TWELVE MONTHS DO YOU THINK THAT BBC2 HAS BECOME BETTER, WORSE OR HAS IT STAYED ABOUT THE SAME?

Universe: All with television
Base: All

				CHANNEL LOYALTY		
	TOTAL	BBC1	BBC2	ITV	CHANNEL 4	NONE
UNWEIGHTED TOTAL	1034	278	40	390	28	298
WEIGHTED TOTAL	1036	276	41	397	25	297
BETTER	149	47	10	49	3	39
	14.%	17.%	26.%	12.%	13.%	13.%
WORSE	54	9	3	23	4	14
	5.%	3.%	8.%	6.%	17.%	5.%
ABOUT THE SAME	669	187	27	236	14	205
	65.%	68.%	67.%	60.%	54.%	69.%
NEVER WATCH	48	5	-	30	1	12
	5.%	2.%	-	8.%	4.%	4.%
DON'T KNOW	116	27	-	58	3	28
	11.%	10.%	-	15.%	13.%	10.%

Q. OVER THE LAST TWELVE MONTHS DO YOU THINK ITV HAS BECOME BETTER, WORSE OR HAS IT STAYED ABOUT THE SAME?

Universe: All with television
Base: All

				CHANNEL LOYALTY		
	TOTAL	BBC1	BBC2	ITV	CHANNEL 4	NONE
UNWEIGHTED TOTAL	1034	278	40	390	28	298
WEIGHTED TOTAL	1036	276	41	397	25	297
BETTER	151	24	3	94	2	27
	15.%	9.%	8.%	24.%	8.%	9.%
WORSE	127	45	10	34	4	34
	12.%	16.%	26.%	8.%	17.%	11.%
ABOUT THE SAME	703	183	25	262	17	216
	68.%	66.%	62.%	66.%	67.%	73.%
NEVER WATCH	13	7	1	2	-	2
	1.%	3.%	3.%	1.%	-	1.%
DON'T KNOW	42	17	1	4	2	18
	4.%	6.%	3.%	1.%	8.%	6.%

contd.

TABLE 38
contd.
Q. OVER THE LAST TWELVE MONTHS DO YOU THINK THAT CHANNEL 4 HAS
BECOME BETTER, WORSE OR HAS IT STAYED ABOUT THE SAME?

Universe: All with television
Base: All

		CHANNEL LOYALTY				
	TOTAL	BBC1	BBC2	ITV	CHANNEL 4	NONE
UNWEIGHTED TOTAL	1034	278	40	390	28	298
WEIGHTED TOTAL	1036	276	41	397	25	297
BETTER	451	122	24	168	15	123
	44.%	44.%	59.%	42.%	58.%	41.%
WORSE	46	12	2	21	1	10
	4.%	4.%	5.%	5.%	4.%	4.%
ABOUT THE SAME	355	79	12	141	9	114
	34.%	29.%	28.%	35.%	38.%	39.%
NEVER WATCH	51	17	-	24	-	10
	5.%	6.%	-	6.%	-	4.%
DON'T KNOW	132	47	3	43	-	39
	13.%	17.%	8.%	11.%	-	13.%

Q. OVER THE LAST TWELVE MONTHS DO YOU THINK THAT BBC1 HAS BECOME
BETTER, WORSE OR HAS IT STAYED ABOUT THE SAME?

Universe: All with television
Base: All

		CHANNEL LOYALTY				
	TOTAL	BBC1	BBC2	ITV	CHANNEL 4	NONE
UNWEIGHTED TOTAL	1034	278	40	390	28	298
WEIGHTED TOTAL	1036	276	41	397	25	297
BETTER	190	64	4	79	3	40
	18.%	23.%	10.%	20.%	13.%	13.%
WORSE	157	42	12	48	6	49
	15.%	15.%	28.%	12.%	25.%	17.%
ABOUT THE SAME	643	166	25	248	14	191
	62.%	60.%	62.%	62.%	54.%	64.%
NEVER WATCH	8	-	-	6	1	1
	1.%	-	-	2.%	4.%	*
DON'T KNOW	37	4	-	16	1	16
	4.%	2.%	-	4.%	4.%	5.%

* = less than .5

TABLE 39

Q. WHICH CHANNEL DO YOU THINK IS MOST LIKELY TO SHOW: PLAYS INVOLVING BAD LANGUAGE OR EXPLICIT SEX SCENES?

Universe: All with television
Base: All

	TOTAL	BBC1	BBC2	ITV	CHANNEL 4	NONE
				CHANNEL LOYALTY		
UNWEIGHTED TOTAL	1034	278	40	390	28	298
WEIGHTED TOTAL	1036	276	41	397	25	297
BBC 1	108	29	6	42	3	27
	10.%	11.%	15.%	11.%	13.%	9.%
BBC 2	103	26	2	38	1	36
	10.%	10.%	5.%	10.%	4.%	12.%
ITV	232	68	18	90	2	54
	22.%	25.%	44.%	23.%	8.%	18.%
CHANNEL 4	537	144	19	212	18	145
	52.%	52.%	46.%	53.%	71.%	49.%
NO DIFFERENCE	141	38	6	46	3	47
	14.%	14.%	15.%	12.%	13.%	16.%
DON'T KNOW	98	31	1	34	-	31
	9.%	11.%	3.%	8.%	-	11.%

TABLE 40

Q. WHICH CHANNEL DO YOU THINK IS LIKELY TO SHOW: POLITICAL SATIRE?

Universe: All with television
Base: All

	TOTAL	BBC1	BBC2	ITV	CHANNEL 4	NONE
				CHANNEL LOYALTY		
UNWEIGHTED TOTAL	1034	278	40	390	28	298
WEIGHTED TOTAL	1036	276	41	397	25	297
BBC 1	217	52	5	96	7	57
	21.%	19.%	13.%	24.%	29.%	19.%
BBC 2	276	90	13	99	5	69
	27.%	33.%	31.%	25.%	21.%	23.%
ITV	190	46	14	65	7	58
	18.%	17.%	33.%	16.%	29.%	19.%
CHANNEL 4	205	57	6	70	7	64
	20.%	21.%	15.%	18.%	29.%	22.%
NO DIFFERENCE	86	24	2	26	1	33
	8.%	9.%	5.%	7.%	4.%	11.%
DON'T KNOW	114	26	2	54	-	33
	11.%	10.%	5.%	13.%	-	11.%

contd.

TABLE 40
contd.

Q. WHICH CHANNEL DO YOU THINK IS MOST LIKELY TO SHOW: COMEDY SHOWS THAT POKE FUN AT MEMBERS OF THE GOVERNMENT?

Universe: All with television
Base: All

	TOTAL	CHANNEL LOYALTY				
		BBC1	BBC2	ITV	CHANNEL 4	NONE
UNWEIGHTED TOTAL	1034	278	40	390	28	298
WEIGHTED TOTAL	1036	276	41	397	25	297
BBC 1	178	52	9	57	3	57
	17.%	19.%	23.%	14.%	13.%	19.%
BBC 2	119	50	5	27	4	31
	11.%	18.%	13.%	7.%	17.%	11.%
ITV	514	123	19	234	12	127
	50.%	44.%	46.%	59.%	46.%	43.%
CHANNEL 4	134	36	6	42	6	44
	13.%	13.%	15.%	11.%	25.%	15.%
NO DIFFERENCE	109	31	3	38	3	34
	11.%	11.%	8.%	10.%	13.%	11.%
DON'T KNOW	107	25	2	40	2	38
	10.%	9.%	5.%	10.%	8.%	13.%

TABLE 41

Q. WHICH CHANNEL DO YOU THINK IS MOST LIKELY TO SHOW: DOCUMENTARIES ABOUT SOCIAL ISSUES SUCH AS INNER CITY RIOTS?

Universe: All with television
Base: All

	TOTAL	CHANNEL LOYALTY				
		BBC1	BBC2	ITV	CHANNEL 4	NONE
UNWEIGHTED TOTAL	1034	278	40	390	28	298
WEIGHTED TOTAL	1036	276	41	397	25	297
BBC 1	308	96	6	120	4	82
	30.%	35.%	15.%	30.%	17.%	28.%
BBC 2	277	87	17	98	5	70
	27.%	32.%	41.%	25.%	21.%	24.%
ITV	232	63	7	91	7	63
	22.%	23.%	18.%	23.%	29.%	21.%
CHANNEL 4	156	38	12	45	9	52
	15.%	14.%	28.%	11.%	38.%	18.%
NO DIFFERENCE	106	19	4	41	1	41
	10.%	7.%	10.%	10.%	4.%	14.%
DON'T KNOW	73	17	1	31	1	23
	7.%	6.%	3.%	8.%	4.%	8.%

contd.

TABLE 41
contd.

Q. WHICH CHANNEL DO YOU THINK IS MOST LIKELY TO SHOW: INVESTIGATION PROGRAMMES SHOWING CORRUPTION IN HIGH PLACES?

Universe: All with television
Base: All

	TOTAL	BBC1	BBC2	ITV	CHANNEL 4	NONE
					CHANNEL LOYALTY	
UNWEIGHTED TOTAL	1034	278	40	390	28	298
WEIGHTED TOTAL	1036	276	41	397	25	297
BBC 1	326	106	15	118	8	80
	32.%	38.%	36.%	30.%	33.%	27.%
BBC 2	160	37	9	60	3	50
	15.%	13.%	23.%	15.%	13.%	17.%
ITV	269	69	10	119	7	63
	26.%	25.%	26.%	30.%	29.%	21.%
CHANNEL 4	79	14	6	30	6	22
	8.%	5.%	15.%	8.%	25.%	7.%
NO DIFFERENCE	144	38	4	42	3	57
	14.%	14.%	10.%	11.%	13.%	19.%
DON'T KNOW	165	43	1	65	1	55
	16.%	16.%	3.%	16.%	4.%	18.%

Q. WHICH CHANNEL DO YOU THINK IS MOST LIKELY TO SHOW: DOCUMENTARIES ABOUT CORRUPTION IN BIG BUSINESS?

	TOTAL	BBC1	BBC2	ITV	CHANNEL 4	NONE
					CHANNEL LOYALTY	
UNWEIGHTED TOTAL	1034	278	40	390	28	298
WEIGHTED TOTAL	1036	276	41	397	25	297
BBC 1	323	97	12	120	5	90
	31.%	35.%	28.%	30.%	21.%	30.%
BBC 2	199	54	14	72	6	54
	19.%	19.%	33.%	18.%	25.%	18.%
ITV	229	49	9	102	8	60
	22.%	18.%	23.%	26.%	33.%	20.%
CHANNEL 4	77	24	7	23	5	17
	7.%	9.%	18.%	6.%	21.%	6.%
NO DIFFERENCE	149	38	5	49	3	54
	14.%	14.%	13.%	12.%	13.%	18.%
DON'T KNOW	186	46	2	75	3	60
	18.%	17.%	5.%	19.%	13.%	20.%

TABLE 42

Q. WHICH CHANNEL DO YOU THINK IS MOST LIKELY TO SHOW INTERVIEWS WITH TERRORISTS SUCH AS THE IRA?

Universe: All with television
Base: All

| | TOTAL | CHANNEL LOYALTY | | | | |
		BBC1	BBC2	ITV	CHANNEL 4	NONE
UNWEIGHTED TOTAL	1034	278	40	390	28	298
WEIGHTED TOTAL	1036	276	41	397	25	297
BBC 1	273	73	16	112	7	64
	26.%	27.%	38.%	28.%	29.%	22.%
BBC 2	128	39	5	47	4	33
	12.%	14.%	13.%	12.%	17.%	11.%
ITV	293	76	15	116	4	82
	28.%	27.%	36.%	29.%	17.%	28.%
CHANNEL 4	127	41	3	39	6	38
	12.%	15.%	8.%	10.%	25.%	13.%
NO DIFFERENCE	143	34	2	47	3	57
	14.%	12.%	5.%	12.%	13.%	19.%
DON'T KNOW	152	41	2	62	3	44
	15.%	15.%	5.%	16.%	13.%	15.%

TABLE 43

Q. DURING A CRISIS SUCH AS THE FALKLANDS CONFLICT DO YOU THINK TELEVISION CURRENT AFFAIRS PROGRAMMES SHOULD CRITICISE THE GOVERNMENT'S HANDLING OF THE CONFLICT IF THEY THINK IT IS NECESSARY, OR SHOULD THEY AVOID CRITICISING THE GOVERNMENT?

Universe: All with television
Base: All

| | TOTAL | CHANNEL LOYALTY | | | | |
		BBC1	BBC2	ITV	CHANNEL 4	NONE
UNWEIGHTED TOTAL	1034	278	40	390	28	298
WEIGHTED TOTAL	1036	276	41	397	25	297
SHOULD CRITICISE	610	156	28	225	16	185
	59.%	57.%	69.%	57.%	63.%	62.%
AVOID CRITICISM	349	98	13	142	7	90
	34.%	35.%	31.%	36.%	29.%	30.%
DON'T KNOW	77	22	-	30	2	22
	7.%	8.%	-	8.%	8.%	7.%

contd.

TABLE 43
contd.

Q. IN NORMAL CIRCUMSTANCES WHERE THERE IS NO NATIONAL CRISIS DO YOU THINK TELEVISION CURRENT AFFAIRS PROGRAMMES SHOULD CRITICISE GOVERNMENT ACTIONS IF THEY THINK IT IS NECESSARY OR SHOULD THEY AVOID CRITICISING THE GOVERNMENT?

Universe: All with television
Base: All

	TOTAL	CHANNEL LOYALTY				
		BBC1	BBC2	ITV	CHANNEL 4	NONE
UNWEIGHTED TOTAL	1034	278	40	390	28	298
WEIGHTED TOTAL	1036	276	41	397	25	297
SHOULD CRITICISE	777	215	35	274	21	232
	75.%	78.%	85.%	69.%	83.%	78.%
AVOID CRITICISM	184	42	6	86	4	45
	18.%	15.%	15.%	22.%	17.%	15.%
DON'T KNOW	76	19	-	37	-	20
	7.%	7.%	-	9.%	-	7.%

TABLE 44

Q. WHICH OF THE FOUR CHANNELS DO YOU THINK WOULD BE MOST LIKELY TO CRITICISE THE GOVERNMENT'S HANDLING OF AN ISSUE?

Universe: All with television
Base: All

	TOTAL	CHANNEL LOYALTY				
		BBC1	BBC2	ITV	CHANNEL 4	NONE
UNWEIGHTED TOTAL	1034	278	40	390	28	298
WEIGHTED TOTAL	1036	276	41	397	25	297
BBC 1	188	49	13	73	5	47
	18.%	18.%	31.%	19.%	21.%	16.%
BBC 2	62	17	4	21	4	16
	6.%	6.%	10.%	5.%	17.%	5.%
ITV	233	59	7	109	4	54
	22.%	21.%	18.%	28.%	17.%	18.%
CHANNEL 4	92	29	3	21	8	30
	9.%	11.%	8.%	5.%	33.%	10.%
NO DIFFERENCE	375	107	15	128	4	121
	36.%	39.%	36.%	32.%	17.%	41.%
DON'T KNOW	128	26	1	59	1	41
	12.%	10.%	3.%	15.%	4.%	14.%

TABLE 45

Q. WHICH OF THE FOUR CHANNELS DO YOU THINK WOULD BE LEAST LIKELY
TO CRITICISE THE GOVERNMENT'S HANDLING OF AN ISSUE?

Universe: All with television
Base: All

		CHANNEL LOYALTY				
	TOTAL	BBC1	BBC2	ITV	CHANNEL 4	NONE
UNWEIGHTED TOTAL	1034	278	40	390	28	298
WEIGHTED TOTAL	1036	276	41	397	25	297
BBC 1	200	62	7	75	6	50
	19.%	22.%	18.%	19.%	25.%	17.%
BBC 2	126	38	6	43	5	34
	12.%	14.%	15.%	11.%	21.%	11.%
ITV	83	19	3	31	3	26
	8.%	7.%	8.%	8.%	13.%	9.%
CHANNEL 4	96	18	7	46	3	21
	9.%	6.%	18.%	12.%	13.%	7.%
NO DIFFERENCE	379	108	14	128	6	123
	37.%	39.%	33.%	32.%	25.%	41.%
DON'T KNOW	177	41	5	79	3	49
	17.%	15.%	13.%	20.%	13.%	17.%

TABLE 46

Q. WHY DO YOU SAY THAT?

Base: All thinking one channel more likely to criticise than the others.

	TOTAL	BBC1	BBC2	ITV	CH 4
UNWEIGHTED TOTAL	544	185	60	239	103
	100.%	34.%	11.%	44.%	19.%
WEIGHTED TOTAL	533	188	62	233	92
	100.%	35.%	12.%	44.%	17.%
HAS MORE OF THAT TYPE OF					
PROGRAMME/MORE CURRENT	140	62	33	40	18
AFFAIRS	26.%	33.%	53.%	17.%	19.%
MORE CRITICISM/MORE OUTSPOKEN/	106	37	5	45	22
NOT AFRAID TO SAY THESE THINGS	20.%	20.%	8.%	19.%	24.%
CHANNEL NOT GOVT RUN/FUNDED/	55	3	1	44	8
CONTROLLED	10.%	2.%	2.%	19.%	9.%
MORE INDEPENDENT/FREEDOM TO	51	2	1	36	14
EXPRESS THEIR VIEWS	10.%	1.%	2.%	15.%	15.%
HAVE SEEN THEM DO IT/OFTEN DO IT/	50	23	5	20	8
CRITICISE GOVT	9.%	12.%	8.%	9.%	9.%
THEY LIKE TO GIVE THE FACTS/MORE	36	18	8	7	6
HONEST/MORE DIRECT	7.%	9.%	14.%	3.%	7.%
CHANNEL RADICAL/LEFT WING/	26	8	1	10	7
SHOWS LEFT WING PROGRAMMES	5.%	4.%	2.%	5.%	8.%
HAVE DEVELOPED AN ANTI-GOVT	17	7	-	8	3
APPROACH	3.%	4.%	-	4.%	3.%
DO NOT WATCH OTHER CHANNEL/	13	8	-	6	-
WATCH THIS CHANNEL MORE	2.%	4.%	-	3.%	-
BBC PRO-GOVERNMENT	13	-	-	13	1
	2.%	-	-	5.%	1.%
OTHER ANSWERS	66	23	7	24	15
	12.%	12.%	12.%	10.%	16.%
DON'T KNOW/NO ANSWER	39	16	4	19	4
	7.%	8.%	7.%	8.%	5.%

TABLE 47

Q. WHY DO YOU SAY THAT?

Base: All thinking one channel less likely to criticise than the others

	TOTAL	BBC1	BBC2	ITV	CH 4
UNWEIGHTED TOTAL	486	207	125	83	96
WEIGHTED TOTAL	480	200	126	83	96
LESS CRITICAL/AVOIDS CRITICISING	69	16	27	14	14
GOVT/MORE CRITICISM ON OTHERS	14.%	8.%	22.%	16.%	14.%
IT IS THE GOVT/PART OF THE GOVT/	12	9	3	-	-
A GOVT AFFAIR	2.%	5.%	3.%	-	-
CHANNEL GOVT RUN/FUNDED/					
CONTROLLED/NEEDS GOVT TO	78	71	16	1	1
SANCTION LICENCES	16.%	36.%	13.%	1.%	1.%
MUST NOT UPSET ADVERTISERS	4	-	-	4	-
	1.%	-	-	5.%	-
HAS LESS OF THAT TYPE OF					
PROGRAMME/LESS NEWS/CURRENT	91	12	28	18	36
AFFAIRS	19.%	6.%	23.%	22.%	37.%
HAS FEW POLITICAL PROGRAMMES/	12	-	6	4	1
AVOIDS POLITICAL PROGRAMMES	2.%	-	5.%	5.%	1.%
FOR THE GOVT/SUPPORTS GOVT	41	33	8	2	-
OF THE DAY	9.%	16.%	7.%	3.%	-
CHANNEL CONSERVATIVE/RIGHT	29	22	4	4	-
WING/PRO-ESTABLISHMENT	6.%	11.%	3.%	5.%	-
MORE HIGHBROW/INTELLECTUAL	10	-	9	1	-
CHANNEL	2.%	-	8.%	1.%	-
LIGHTER/MORE ENTERTAINING	27	1	-	17	9
CHANNEL	6.%	1.%	-	20.%	10.%
HAS WIDER SPECTRUM OF	8	1	-	6	1
PROGRAMMES WITH LESS DEPTH	2.%	1.%	-	8.%	1.%
I HAVE NOT SEEN THEM DO IT	39	12	9	5	15
[CRITICISE]	8.%	6.%	8.%	6.%	15.%
OTHER ANSWERS	75	29	23	19	8
	16.%	15.%	18.%	23.%	9.%
DON'T KNOW	38	16	6	4	13
	8.%	8.%	5.%	5.%	13.%

TABLE 48

Q. IF THE BBC WAS GOING TO SHOW A PROGRAMME ABOUT TERRORISTS AND RECEIVED LOTS OF COMPLAINTS FROM THE PUBLIC SAYING IT SHOULD NOT BE SHOWN, HOW MUCH ATTENTION DO YOU THINK THE BBC WOULD PAY TO THESE COMPLAINTS?

Universe: All with television
Base: All

		CHANNEL LOYALTY				
	TOTAL	BBC1	BBC2	ITV	CHANNEL 4	NONE
UNWEIGHTED TOTAL	1034	278	40	390	28	298
WEIGHTED TOTAL	1036	276	41	397	25	297
A GREAT DEAL	163	46	5	55	7	49
	16.%	17.%	13.%	14.%	29.%	17.%
A FAIR AMOUNT	387	115	23	122	7	120
	37.%	42.%	56.%	31.%	29.%	40.%
A LITTLE	270	65	12	116	4	72
	26.%	24.%	28.%	29.%	17.%	24.%
NONE AT ALL	168	36	1	83	4	44
	16.%	13.%	3.%	21.%	17.%	15.%
DON'T KNOW	48	14	-	21	2	12
	5.%	5.%	-	5.%	8.%	4.%

TABLE 49

Q. IF ITV WAS GOING TO SHOW A PROGRAMME ABOUT TERRORISTS AND RECEIVED LOTS OF COMPLAINTS FROM THE PUBLIC SAYING IT SHOULD NOT BE SHOWN, HOW MUCH ATTENTION DO YOU THINK ITV WOULD PAY TO THESE COMPLAINTS?

Universe: All with television
Base: All

		CHANNEL LOYALTY				
	TOTAL	BBC1	BBC2	ITV	CHANNEL 4	NONE
UNWEIGHTED TOTAL	1034	278	40	390	28	298
WEIGHTED TOTAL	1036	276	41	397	25	297
A GREAT DEAL	129	39	4	40	5	41
	12.%	14.%	10.%	10.%	21.%	14.%
A FAIR AMOUNT	357	101	21	116	7	111
	34.%	37.%	51.%	29.%	29.%	37.%
A LITTLE	315	82	14	127	6	86
	30.%	30.%	33.%	32.%	25.%	29.%
NONE AT ALL	178	40	1	88	5	44
	17.%	14.%	3.%	22.%	21.%	15.%
DON'T KNOW	57	15	1	25	1	15
	5.%	5.%	3.%	6.%	4.%	5.%

* = less than .5

74

APPENDICES

APPENDIX I

NOP DECEMBER 1984   Quota Telephone National 1,006

'The BBC is proposing to put up the cost of a TV licence from £46 to about £70. Some people have suggested that it would be a good idea for the BBC to take advertisements in order to avoid putting up the licence fee. With that in mind I'd like you to tell me how much you agree or disagree with these statements.'

'I would be happier if the BBC took advertisements than if they put up the licence fee':

Agree strongly	52%
Agree to some extent	18%
Neither agree nor disagree	6%
Disagree to some extent	9%
Disagree strongly	13%
Don't know	2%

MORI December 1984   Ad Hoc Quota National 1,060

'The BBC has recently announced that it cannot maintain its current level of radio and TV services with the income it gets at present from TV licences. Which of the following solutions to this problem do you favour?'

SHOWCARD

Increase the cost of a TV licence and maintain the present service	14%
Keep the cost of a TV licence as it is and cut back the service	14%
Keep the cost of a TV licence as it is but introduce some advertising on BBC to maintain the present level of service	69%
Don't know	3%

MORI August 1985   Ad Hoc Quota National 1083

'Thinking about how the BBC is financed, which of the following would you personally prefer?'

All financed from compulsory licence fee as at present	27%
Some financed from compulsory licence fee, some from advertising	31%
All financed from advertising	31%
All financed from a voluntary subscription which meant only those who paid the fee would receive BBC programmes	7%

MORI August 1985   Omnibus Quota National 1,016

'Would you favour or oppose the abolition of the TV licence fee and its replacement with commercial advertising on BBC television?'

Favour	65%
Oppose	30%
Don't know	5%

MORI October 1985 Omnibus Quota National 2,068

'As you know, the BBC is currently financed by the licence fee. Future increases in revenue could be raised by allowing some advertising as well. Generally speaking, would you prefer advertising to be allowed on BBC radio and television provided it is properly regulated or do you think advertising should not be allowed under any circumstances on BBC radio or television?'

Willing to allow advertising on BBC	67%
Would not allow under any circumstances	29%
Don't know	4%

NOP (Peacock) November 1985 Ad Hoc Random National 1,990

SHOWCARD C
'Which of these statements is closest to your view?'

In favour of advertising providing quality of programmes is not lower	53%
In favour of advertising whether quality is lower or not	13%
Opposed to advertising whether quality of programmes is lower or not	31%
Don't know	3%

Questions About Advertising on the BBC

MORI March 1984 Ad Hoc Quota National 1,000

'The BBC has recently announced that it cannot maintain its current level of radio and TV services with the income it gets at present from TV licences. Which of the following solutions to this problem do you favour?'

SHOWCARD

Increase the cost of TV licence and maintain the present service	13%
Keep the cost of the TV licence as it is and cut back the service	12%
Keep the cost of a TV licence as it is but introduce some advertising on BBC to maintain the present level of service	69%
Don't know	6%

GALLUP November 1984 Omnibus National

'Would you approve or disapprove if BBC television were to accept commercial advertising as a means of funding its services?'

Approve	66%
Disapprove	25%
Don't know	9%

'The BBC is proposing to put up the cost of a colour television licence from £46 to about £70. Some people have suggested that it would be a good idea for the BBC to take advertising in order to avoid putting up the licence fee. Do you agree or disagree that it would be a good idea for the BBC to avoid putting up the cost of a television licence by taking advertising?'

Agree strongly	48%
Agree	22%
Disagree	11%
Disagree strongly	17%
Don't know	1%

APPENDIX II

The Research – Qualitative
A total of eighteen group discussions were organised and spread as best as resources would allow around the country: six each were held in the North, Midlands and the South, and structured by age, class and sex. Two techniques were employed. An attitude scale questionnaire was used, followed by in-depth, semi-structured discussions lasting between forty-five to seventy-five minutes. The intention of the discussions was to allow the participants opportunity to express their views and enlarge on the issues in the attitude questionnaire. The answers received from the questionnaire itself were factor analysed.

Our main survey, administered for us by NOP, attempted to advance on previous surveys by investigating underlying attitudes to broadcasting and to get respondents to consider and react to the possible consequences of any change in the structure of British broadcasting. Once the questionnaire was drawn up it was tested in a small-scale pilot survey. Four interviewers each conducted six interviews between February 27th and March 2nd. Following the pilot a number of alterations were made to the questionnaire. A final version of the questionnaire was then drawn up.

The Research – Quantitative
The survey was conducted with a probability sample (a 'random' sample) in 90 constituencies across Great Britain. The constituencies were chosen with probability proportional to size from a multi-stage stratified list of all constituencies in Great Britain, the variables for stratification being region, urban/rural mix and the social class profile. In each constituency a single polling district was selected for the survey. From a random start point every fifteenth elector's name was underlined, until 20 names had been selected in each constituency (22 names in each GLC constituency).

No substitutes were allowed for the selected elector, but there was a procedure for interviewing non-electors. Wherever an interviewer found someone aged 18 or over living at the same address as the selected elector, but who was not on the electoral register, then all non-electors aged 18 and over at the address were listed and one selected for interview according to a randomised procedure.

Whilst all electors had an equal chance of selection, non-electors had a variable chance of selection based on two factors. The greater the number of electors at any address the greater the chance was of that address being selected for the survey, and the greater the chance of non-electors at the address entering the selection procedure. However, the greater the number of non-electors at an address the lower the chance was of any individual non-elector being selected for the survey. Thus in the data analysis all non-electors received a weight of:

$$\frac{\text{the number of non-electors at the address}}{\text{the number of electors at the address}}$$

Fieldwork
Interviewing took place between March 10th and 23rd 1986, with 90 interviewers working on the survey, one in each sampling point. The total number of interviews completed was 1061, and this represents an overall contact rate of 61%. The detailed breakdown of contact rate is as follows:

Elector Sample

Electors selected	1822
Address empty/demolished	45
Elector moved/died	242
Electors available for interview	1535
Electors interviewed	928
Elector contact rate	60.5%

Non-elector Sample

Non-electors identified	205
Non-electors interviewed	133
Non-elector contact rate	64.9%

Total Sample

Available for interview	1740
Interviewed	1061
Overall contact rate	61.0%

Analysis

Code frames were drawn up for the two open-ended questions, Q83 and Q85, and in addition a list of programmes was developed for the favourite and low quality programmes at Q22 and Q40. At these two questions the coding team also recorded whether the respondent had been correct or incorrect in allocating each programme to its channel.

Several composite variables were used in the analysis and these are explained below:

a) TV viewing
Mid-point values were assigned to the answers at Q12 and Q14. The Q14 score was multiplied by the Q13 score to give total weekday hours. This was added to the weekend viewing hours at Q12 to produce a composite total hours. Respondents were then split into three terciles based on total hours watched and the terciles designated as heavy, medium and light.

b) Channel knowledge
Each respondent was classified as having correctly identified all the programmes they named at Q22 and Q40, having correctly identified some of the programmes they named, or none of the programmes named. Where respondents gave generic answers rather than actual programmes – 'the news', 'sports' and so on – these were not scored as either correct or incorrect.

c) Channel loyalty
Defined as the channel watched most often (Q18).

d) Cut hours
Opposition or support for the idea of cutting the total number of hours of television (Q35).

e) Commitment to public service broadcasting
Scores were given to each respondent as follows:

Q75		Score 1.5 for 'pay more', score 4.5 for 'pay some'
Q77	i)	Score from 1 for definitely agree to 5 for definitely disagree
	ii)	Score from 5 for definitely agree to 1 for definitely disagree
	iii)	Score from 5 for definitely agree to 1 for definitely disagree
	iv)	Score from 1 for definitely agree to 5 for definitely disagree
	v)	Score from 1 for definitely agree to 5 for definitely disagree

Scores were then summarised as follows:

Low commitment	up to 17
Medium commitment	17.5 – 20
High commitment	20.5 – 22.5
Very high commitment	23.0 – 29.5

APPENDIX III

FACTOR ANALYSIS

FACTOR	EIGENVALUE	PCT OF VAR	CUM PCT
1	4.86962	13.2	13.2
2	3.66072	9.9	23.1
3	2.51425	6.8	29.9
4	1.92792	5.2	35.1

	FACTOR 1	FACTOR 2	FACTOR 3	FACTOR 4
Q12	-0.72286	-0.12202	.05521	-0.08303
Q5	.60338	.30437	-0.05130	.27333
Q8	.58524	-0.10300	.39896	-0.13720
Q4	.54546	.02220	.39592	-0.00225
Q6	.49388	.12742	.03588	-0.18786
Q29	.49114	.36140	-0.00849	-0.16375
Q19	-0.48916	.12736	-0.22377	.06141
Q2	-0.46866	.46409	-0.17826	.02278
Q24	.40675	-0.11915	-0.20022	.03555
Q36	.01984	.68109	.04608	-0.13488
Q27	.04346	.57004	.33274	.25369
Q22	-0.08392	.56383	-0.01430	.03550
Q34	.05629	.50335	.23781	-0.24846
Q35	.28298	.50045	-0.00477	.28602
Q28	.26098	.49309	.19545	-0.06486
Q17	.26093	.45577	-0.29748	-0.07606
Q18	.14130	.35039	-0.06627	.27092
Q9	.08688	-0.33308	-0.28240	.17621
Q37	.12367	.16057	.65965	.02879
Q20	.15518	.23271	.63602	-0.07310
Q26	-0.00773	.02267	.57601	.12245
Q3	.04124	.00737	.56596	.09864
Q1	-0.20533	-0.47259	.52601	-0.23498
Q31	.34449	.26223	.49860	-0.25500
Q32	.06252	-0.14524	.49181	-0.20729
Q21	.23253	.24356	-0.40010	.25261
Q10	.08429	.04596	-0.00037	.67072
Q15	-0.12883	.02493	-0.13189	.55049
Q23	.37544	.13636	.08951	-0.47501
Q16	.03800	-0.08530	.06028	.40361
Q14	.36117	.25325	.09643	.36362
Q13	.04776	.16750	-0.13556	-0.28065
Q11	.18424	-0.16229	.04773	-0.23636
Q7	.13037	-0.04972	.05182	.11100
Q33	.07954	.21420	.21684	-0.12825
Q30	.02587	.22836	-0.08095	.13697
Q25	-0.31818	.24243	.06895	.02791

AGREE SCALE QUESTIONS

Please circle the relevant number.

1) The licence fee is good value for money.
    Strongly agree 1
    Agree 2
    No opinion 3
    Disagree 4
    Strongly disagree 5

2) It would be good to have more channels to watch instead of just 4 as at
   present.
    Strongly agree 1
    Agree 2
    No opinion 3
    Disagree 4
    Strongly disagree 5

3) The BBC has made Britain respected around the world.
    Strongly agree 1
    Agree 2
    No opinion 3
    Disagree 4
    Strongly disagree 5

4) Adverts spoil the pleasure of television.
    Strongly agree 1
    Agree 2
    No opinion 3
    Disagree 4
    Strongly disagree 5

5) It's wrong for the BBC to have breakfast television when it complains it
   hasn't the money to finance the existing service.
    Strongly agree 1
    Agree 2
    No opinion 3
    Disagree 4
    Strongly disagree 5

6) BBC should not be making soap operas such as EastEnders.
    Strongly agree 1
    Agree 2
    No opinion 3
    Disagree 4
    Strongly disagree 5

7) I watch too much TV.
    Strongly agree 1
    Agree 2
    No opinion 3
    Disagree 4
    Strongly disagree 5

8) Adverts would make the BBC too commercial.

Strongly agree 1
Agree 2
No opinion 3
Disagree 4
Strongly disagree 5

9) There is very little difference between the quality of programmes shown on BBC1 and ITV.

Strongly agree 1
Agree 2
No opinion 3
Disagree 4
Strongly disagree 5

10) I don't like serious programmes.

Strongly agree 1
Agree 2
No opinion 3
Disagree 4
Strongly disagree 5

11) I don't like alternative comedy.

Strongly agree 1
Agree 2
No opinion 3
Disagree 4
Strongly disagree 5

12) I think breakfast TV is a good idea.

Strongly agree 1
Agree 2
No opinion 3
Disagree 4
Strongly disagree 5

13) If I feel like watching TV I can watch some pretty bad stuff.

Strongly agree 1
Agree 2
No opinion 3
Disagree 4
Strongly disagree 5

14) If you can't afford to pay for something I don't think you should get it on credit.

Strongly agree 1
Agree 2
No opinion 3
Disagree 4
Strongly disagree 5

15) *Panorama* is boring.

    Strongly agree 1
    Agree 2
    No opinion 3
    Disagree 4
    Strongly disagree 5

16) I'd be lost without TV.

    Strongly agree 1
    Agree 2
    No opinion 3
    Disagree 4
    Strongly disagree 5

17) The standard of programmes on TV is worse now than when I first got a set.

    Strongly agree 1
    Agree 2
    No opinion 3
    Disagree 4
    Strongly disagree 5

18) Poor people should not have to pay the full licence fee.

    Strongly agree 1
    Agree 2
    No opinion 3
    Disagree 4
    Strongly disagree 5

19) Adverts on TV are fun.

    Strongly agree 1
    Agree 2
    No opinion 3
    Disagree 4
    Strongly disagree 5

20) If it wasn't for the BBC British TV would be awful.

    Strongly agree 1
    Agree 2
    No opinion 3
    Disagree 4
    Strongly disagree 5

21) I think it's wrong if someone can prove they never watch BBC TV or listen to BBC Radio that they still have to pay the licence fee.

    Strongly agree 1
    Agree 2
    No opinion 3
    Disagree 4
    Strongly disagree 5

22) TV should be more experimental.
    Strongly agree 1
    Agree 2
    No opinion 3
    Disagree 4
    Strongly disagree 5

23) There are too many imported American programmes on TV.
    Strongly agree 1
    Agree 2
    No opinion 3
    Disagree 4
    Strongly disagree 5

24) Reading is a more valuable activity than watching TV.
    Strongly agree 1
    Agree 2
    No opinion 3
    Disagree 4
    Strongly disagree 5

25) I don't have as much time to watch TV as I would like.
    Strongly agree 1
    Agree 2
    No opinion 3
    Disagree 4
    Strongly disagree 5

26) British TV is the best in the world.
    Strongly agree 1
    Agree 2
    No opinion 3
    Disagree 4
    Strongly disagree 5

27) Current affairs programmes should always be critical of those in power.
    Strongly agree 1
    Agree 2
    No opinion 3
    Disagree 4
    Strongly disagree 5

28) The BBC should leave chat shows to ITV and concentrate on more serious programmes.
    Strongly agree 1
    Agree 2
    No opinion 3
    Disagree 4
    Strongly disagree 5

29) TV should concentrate on making better programmes instead of increasing the number of broadcasting hours.

     Strongly agree 1
     Agree 2
     No opinion 3
     Disagree 4
     Strongly disagree 5

30) It would do people in BBC TV good to have to make a profit.

     Strongly agree 1
     Agree 2
     No opinion 3
     Disagree 4
     Strongly disagree 5

31) ITV is more concerned about making a profit than providing a good service.

     Strongly agree 1
     Agree 2
     No opinion 3
     Disagree 4
     Strongly disagree 5

32) There should be a higher licence fee rather than advertising on BBC.

     Strongly agree 1
     Agree 2
     No opinion 3
     Disagree 4
     Strongly disagree 5

33) I often enjoy the foreign films on TV with sub-titles.

     Strongly agree 1
     Agree 2
     No opinion 3
     Disagree 4
     Strongly disagree 5

34) I make a special effort to watch programmes that have exceptional educational or cultural value.

     Strongly agree 1
     Agree 2
     No opinion 3
     Disagree 4
     Strongly disagree 5

35) TV should just produce what most people like and not bother with programmes for those with special interests or tastes.

     Strongly agree 1
     Agree 2
     No opinion 3
     Disagree 4
     Strongly disagree 5

36) There should be a broader range of programmes on television.

  Strongly agree 1
  Agree 2
  No opinion 3
  Disagree 4
  Strongly disagree 5

37) We must protect the BBC at all costs.

  Strongly agree 1
  Agree 2
  No opinion 3
  Disagree 4
  Strongly disagree 5

The Broadcasting Research Unit is an independent body jointly sponsored by the BBC, BFI, IBA and the Markle Foundation of New York. The BBC, IBA and the Markle Foundation provide finance for the Unit. The BFI houses the Unit and provides administrative support.

Chairman: Dr Richard Hoggart   Head of Unit: Dr Michael Tracey

Broadcasting Research Unit
127 Charing Cross Road
London WC2H OEA

October 1986